ROADSIDE CROSSES
IN CONTEMPORARY MEMORIAL CULTURE

ROADSIDE CROSSES
in Contemporary Memorial Culture

by
Holly Everett

University of North Texas Press
Denton, Texas

The paper in this book meets the minimum requirements of the
American National Standard for Permanence of Paper for Printed
Library Materials, Z39.48.1984

Permissions
University of North Texas Press
PO Box 311336
Denton, TX 76203-1336
940-565-2142

Library of Congress Cataloging-in-Publication Data

Everett, Holly J., 1968–
    Roadside crosses in contemporary memorial culture / by Holly
J. Everett. — 1st ed.
        p.   cm.
    Includes bibliographical references and index.
    ISBN 1-57441-150-0 (cloth : alk. paper)
    1. Crosses. 2. Roadside architecture. 3. Funeral rites and
ceremonies. 4. Death—Social aspects. 5. Crosses—Texas—Austin
Region. 6. Roadside architecture—Texas—Austin Region.
7. Funeral rites and ceremonies—Texas—Austin Region.
8. Death—Social aspects—Texas—Austin Region. 9. Austin
(Tex.)—Social Life and customs. I. Title.
CC305.E84 2002

2002007706

All photos by Holly Everett unless otherwise indicated.
Design by Angela Schmitt

CONTENTS

List of Illustrations

PREFACE

The material presented in this study represents several years of participant-observation, in the sense that I lived in Austin, witnessing the appearance and disappearance of roadside crosses, for seventeen years. I talked about them with friends and relatives, and speculated about their origins, as many of my informants have done. When I mentioned my interest in them to my mother in early 1997, she described one near her home in Austin, and told me that she knew the mother one of the women memorialized at the site.

Shilah Lamay was my first contact. In turn, she referred me to two families who had lost children in automobile accidents. I also spoke to David Canales, who had watched a friend construct a roadside cross for his brother a few years earlier. In other cases, I contacted individuals who had been quoted in newspaper articles, hoping that since they had been willing to speak to a reporter, they would be equally willing to speak to me. As might be expected, a number of interviewees expressed reluctance to open their homes and hearts to a stranger, but in most cases I was treated with a frank openness of spirit that I will never forget.

Primary research was conducted in Texas from April 23 through June 4, 1997, and from December 17 through January 11, 1998. The fieldwork process encompassed library and archival research, directed questionnaires, directive and non-directive tape-recorded interviews, and visual documentation. Crosses throughout the Austin area, as well as the state, were photographed and indexed. Information about individual crosses is based on various combinations of interviews, questionnaires, newspaper articles, and informal conversation.

Holly Everett

Acknowledgments

The work contained in these pages reflects the generosity, patience and memory of a number of people, not only in Texas, but also in Newfoundland. Foremost are my thanks to Vicki and Ronnie Biggs, Susan Crane, Margie Franklin, Shilah Lamay, Jennifer Solter, Thomas Vannatta, and James and Ruby Werchan.

Additionally, Bill Warren and the young adults in his senior English classes provided me with the solid basis upon which I began my fieldwork in Austin. Equally crucial were the interviews granted me by Tom Hurt and Tom Ohlendorf at the Texas Department of Transportation, and Travis County Traffic Engineer Raymond Reed. Photographer Doug Powell shared his many photographs of roadside crosses and grave markers throughout the American southwest. Many other colleagues, friends, and acquaintances assisted by offering their thoughts and opinions on North America's growing number of memorials. Special thanks are due John Bodner, Ryan Britton, Clara Byrne, Catherine DeCent, Jane Gadsby, John Hickman, Julia Kelso, Anne Lafferty, Lara Maynard, Deva McNeill, Andrea O'Brien, and Wendy Welch.

Monetary, scholarly, and moral support from Memorial University of Newfoundland's Department of Folklore sustained me while writing the master's thesis upon which this book is based. Diane Goldstein, Sylvia Grider, Giovanna Del Negro, Leonard Primiano, Paul Smith, and Diane Tye provided references, critical insight and inspiration. I am indebted to Paula Oates at the University of North Texas Press for her editorial assistance.

Finally, I want to acknowledge the unflagging support of my family, and especially my husband, Peter, for which I am extremely grateful.

CHAPTER ONE

Memorial Culture:
The Material Response to Loss

Like most residents of my hometown, Austin, Texas, I took roadside crosses for granted. When I first became conscious of them, as a teenage driver, I thought of them as grim warnings. I did not know then that the crosses had a long history in Mexico and the southwestern United States, nor that they had analogues in several other countries. I had no firsthand knowledge of the construction of those I drove past almost daily. Nonetheless, I found them fascinating and disturbing.

The communicative process of roadside crosses, as tangible evidence of extremely personal pain, inevitably affects an entire community. As centerpieces of fragile, dynamic memorial assemblages, such crosses are only now being examined as more than incidental specks in the cultural landscape of certain groups. A unique form of public, belief-centered material culture, roadside accident markers occupy a rare place not only in the realm of roadside attractions, but in the cognitive map of the individual, a uniqueness that renders them extra-legal, or "outlaw" and almost untouchable markers of liminal space. They represent the continuation and adaptation of one of the oldest forms of memorial culture.

The word "memorial" may first bring to mind civil structures, such as the Lincoln and Vietnam Veterans Memorials in the nation's capitol, and the ceremonies performed at these monuments. Other associations may include Memorial Day observances honoring veterans, or the recent observances held world-wide following the September 11 terror attacks in New York City and Washington, D.C. Simultaneously, in an age that has witnessed the unexpected deaths of numerous celebrities and political figures, ranging from the assassinations of John F. Kennedy and Martin Luther King, Jr., to the more recent deaths of John F. Kennedy, Jr., and Diana Spencer, Princess of Wales, the process and physical manifestation of memorialization has become more mutable. In addition to prescribed commemorative practices, such as the establishment of a governmentally maintained site, individuals with varying degrees of connection to the deceased are creating extemporaneous memorial assemblages.

New York City saw the creation of a number of memorial assemblages commemorating the terror attacks of September 11 (Zeitlin and Harlow 2001). Shrines stood at street corners, fire stations, and public parks throughout the city, filled with floral tributes, flags, candles, and photographs, along with notes of thanks, solidarity, and mourning. The fences surrounding United States embassies around the world were transformed by flowers and candles into large-scale memorials.

Similar tributes were left at the site of Princess Diana's fatal crash in August of 1997 on the *Cours la Reine* in Paris. As well, remembrances were left at the gates of Buckingham and Kensington palaces and outside Harrods department store, displays, Adam Gopnik wrote, "that seemed less like funeral tributes than like the contents of some vast piñata filled with party favors, that someone had broken above London" (1997, 36).[1]

The numerous analogous memorials (now often referred to as "spontaneous shrines") arising from a public outpouring of grief for disease, disaster, and crime victims include the roses and notes left at the site of the ill-fated 1999 bonfire at Texas A&M University (Grider 2001); flowers, notes, and candles left at the home of slain Tejano star Selena Quintanilla in 1995; impromptu murder victim memorials in Philadelphia (DeWolf 1996; Primiano 1997); and the stuffed animals, flowers, and notes intertwined in the fence around the ruins of the bombed Alfred P. Murrah Federal Building in Oklahoma City. In each of these instances, structures generally considered part of the public domain—sidewalks, schools and government buildings—were utilized for private and public mourning, as spaces in which to negotiate meaning.

Completed and dedicated in 1982, the Vietnam Veterans Memorial in Washington, D.C. is one of the most widely recognized sites of such negotiation, far removed from the actual scene of devastation. Scholars including geographer Kenneth Foote and labor historian John Bodnar have discussed the origins and eventual construction of the monument, especially noting the embodiment of the "memory debate" in conflicts concerning appropriate design (Bodnar 1992, 1-9). The memorial continues to be a place for remembering and recasting individual and collective impressions. Folklorist Lydia Fish and historian Kristin Ann Hass have documented responses to the site by "pilgrims" who include veterans and relatives of the dead and missing, and their offerings: rosaries, photographs, letters, flowers, poems, pieces of uniforms, and teddy bears. Emotional reactions to the monument can be so powerful that visitors, usually veterans, sometimes find it difficult to approach the wall and instead hang back in a line of trees facing it (Fish 1987, 83-86). Although the site is thousands of miles from the jungles of Asia, its liminality, in terms of landscape, design, and depiction, renders it a powerful reflection of painful memories.

While the Vietnam Veterans Memorial commemorates the horror of those years from a significant distance, thus perhaps providing some degree of emotional safety to pilgrims, memorials marking physical sites of mass death dot the European landscape, the great majority resulting from genocidal actions of the Nazi regime (commemorative sites are also located in Israel and

North America). The differing priorities of each group involved are possible points of contention. Whereas the problem of memory at Auschwitz/Birkenau centers on religious difference (Bartoszewski 1991; Dwork and Pelt 1994; Perlez 1997; Young 1993), at Dachau local officials struggle to incorporate respectful and instructive recognition of past wrongs into a positive civic image, especially in light of the tens of thousands of visitors arriving every year (Young 1983, 69). The way in which Dachau presents itself as a modern town in relation to its past, however, encompasses not only official literature, but also informal communication between residents and visitors, and once visitors return home, between themselves and members of their own communities. It is precisely this type of informal communication and activity, or folklore, centered on an infamous site that often prompts city planners to initiate a governmentally administered memorialization process.

Austin Memorials, Official and Otherwise

The designation of public and private space for memorialization is an especially delicate task in urban areas experiencing explosive growth. The city of Austin and its residents have in recent years grappled with a perceived need to expand and diversify the metropolitan area's economic base in response to the recent instability of major employers in the area, and the desire to preserve the city's unique quality of life as a more manageable, yet sophisticated and liberal municipality. Cleaner, "greener" industries like computer hardware and software developers and manufacturers have been courted by the Chamber of Commerce in an effort to promote growth while protecting the environment, which includes not only ecological concerns, but social issues as well.

The appropriate use of communally utilized space is an ever-present issue in the lively discussion surrounding public works projects such as parks, recreational and convention facilities, and memorial structures. Austin residents and city officials dealt with the task of effectively representing public and private memory in its commemoration of late blues great Stevie Ray Vaughan. Vaughan, who moved to Austin from Dallas, died in a plane crash in August of 1990. Writing in 1991 for the *Austin American-Statesman*, Michael Point described the memorialization process as one accompanied by "spirited debate," which finally ended with the family's decision to install a statue at Auditorium Shores, an outdoor venue at which Vaughan frequently performed (Foote 1997, 74). The city-owned park runs along Town Lake, a section of the Colorado River which flows through downtown Austin. Ceremonially unveiled in 1993, the bronze statue of Vaughan, standing at eight feet and surrounded by a "meditation garden," was made possible through private donations from individuals both in Austin and around the world, while the allocation of space was made by the city (Point 1993). Facing south, away from the river, Vaughan's likeness is often adorned with fresh flowers, guitar picks, and hand-written tributes.

More controversial was the installation in December of 1997, by members of the Park Hills Baptist Church, of 1,500 small crosses in the expansive front grounds of the church at the intersection of Farm to Market Road 2244 and the Mopac Expressway. A placard placed in front of Park Hills's permanent sign read:

FIELD OF CROSSES
IN MEMORY
OF THE 4,110 BABIES
WHO DIE FROM ABORTIONS
IN OUR COUNTRY EVERY DAY!

Symbolizing the fetuses aborted in America, according to church members, the display was planned to coincide with the twenty-fifth anniversary of the Supreme Court decision legalizing abortion in the United States, Roe vs. Wade. The crosses, mentioned to me by several informants, garnered further media attention in mid-January 1998 when the *Austin American-Statesman* reported that several crosses had been uprooted and burned on the church grounds by vandals.

The "field of crosses" and the Stevie Ray Vaughan memorial represent two points on the public/private memory continuum in the Austin area. Although for the most part privately planned and built, both are intended for public consumption and thus placed in high traffic areas. Vaughan's family, together with the city, created a memorial that is accessible to anyone at almost any time. It stands outside the section of Auditorium Shores that is often enclosed by chain link fences for concerts, festivals, or other pay events. Similarly, the members of Park Hills Baptist Church, desiring as many people as possible to see the anti-abortion display, planted the crosses accordingly, at the corner of the church grounds bordered by two heavily traversed highways. In accordance with its intended use, each memorial's location and structure invites a certain level of engagement from the general public. Of the two, the "field of crosses" is the more obvious candidate for on-going debate and negotiation. It was also a unique memorial in that it was temporary, and did not commemorate a specific event or individual.

The Park Hills Baptist Church and the Stevie Ray Vaughan memorials are similar in that they signify events occurring somewhere distant from the memorial site, as does the Vietnam Veterans Memorial. As noted in the case of Holocaust memorials, and that dedicated to the memory of Martin Luther King, Jr., in Memphis, honoring and shaping memory at the physical site of violence involves a different set of challenges. Foote categorizes the choices made in commemoration of site-specific events as obliteration, rectification, designation, and sanctification (1997, 7).

Obliteration entails the complete eradication of any structure or physical feature related to a tragic incident. Closely related to obliteration is rectification, in which the site is returned to its original condition or totally redeveloped.[2] Austin residents have witnessed this process at work in the rectification of numerous traffic accident sites which now bear little or no trace of destruction, and in the University of Texas's response to Charles Whitman's shooting spree from the tower of the Main Building in 1966. Following the latter incident, damage on campus was cleaned and repaired. The observation deck from which Whitman fired was reopened without ceremony the following year, closed again a few years later due to suicides, then reopened to the public in 1999 (Foote 1997, 195, 357). The site of a 1991 robbery, arson, and quadruple homicide at a northwest Austin yogurt shop serves as an example of designation. A bronze memorial marker was installed there in memory of the four young female victims. Prior to the placing of the marker, friends of the women left lighted candles, flowers, and notes in front of the burned-out store (Phillips 1994).

As envisioned by Foote, sanctification involves the creation of sacred space by physical manipulation of the landscape, whether it be the institution of a memorial plaque, garden, or building, and is usually inspired by disaster or heroic death. There are, however, an increasing number of sanctified spaces created in memory of individuals who were neither well known, nor martyrs, in Austin as well as across North America.

The memorial for Ivan Garth Johnson, killed in 1989, provides an example. It combines an existing public structure, a painted mural, graffiti, and offerings (Fig. 1.1). Spray-painted on an overpass support column are the words:

R.I.P. IVAN

FAIR SAILING TALL BOY

IVAN GARTH JOHNSON

1971 - 1989

DON'T DRINK & DRIVE

YOU MIGHT KILL

SOMEONE'S KID

Fig. 1.1 Overpass memorial for Ivan Garth Johnson

Designs accompanying the message include a black dove, strands of ivy—Ivan's nickname was "Ivy"—and a pattern of triangles at the base of the support. Placed at its foot are rocks decorated with shells, cigarettes, and an empty terra-cotta flowerpot. Long-time Austin resident Ryan Britton reported, "every year, they [the family] cut a piece of wood in the shape of a heart or a circle, and glue seashells in the shape of the number of how many years this boy . . . has been gone. I think the "7" and the "9" are still there."

The column upon which the artwork remained untouched over a decade rises up from the Lamar Bridge over the Colorado River, less than half a mile from the Stevie Ray Vaughan memorial.[3] Rush-hour traffic comes to a standstill on the bridge twice every weekday, providing a captive audience for the memorial's affecting message.

All memorials communicate in different ways. A supporter of anti-abortion legislation will, of course, react to the Park Hills Baptist Church display far differently than someone in favor of legalized abortion. A motorist viewing Ivan Garth Johnson's memorial for the first time will likely be more affected than a commuter who regularly traverses the bridge ten times a week. The fact that four informants recited the memorial's poignant message to me word for word, however, attests to its continued power to impress.

Johnson's memorial has certainly passed into the vernacular knowledge of the area, but visitors to the city will not read about his memorial in any tourist literature or guidebook.[4] In addition, neither the informal memorials described above nor institutionally maintained sites are guaranteed veneration as sacred spaces, as monuments of all kinds have been the objects of vandalism, if not outright desecration.[5] Further, whether due to their origin, design or location, some sites become the focus of pilgrimage, as a shrine, while others fall into disrepair and obscurity.

A memorial on Guadalupe Street in Austin, while relatively

new, appeared to have been abandoned and when photographed was almost camouflaged by a thick layer of dead leaves. The rounded tombstone-like metal marker was completely overtaken by rust save for the rectangular plaque bearing the inscription:

SKIA OURA
March 28, 1996 - November 4, 1996
"Taken by our neglegence [sic]"

A crumbling funeral wreath flanked the north side of the marker on an equally rusted stand. As noted by folklorist Thomas Zimmerman with regard to similarly neglected roadside crosses in south central Kentucky, Oura's memorial has perhaps served its purpose for grieving family and friends (1997, 3). Attention and maintenance may have moved from the site of death to the home or cemetery.

Sacred Space and Pilgrimage

Foote states that the United States, from colonial days to the present, has been something of a landscape of disaster and loss, as well as diversity and beauty, thereby forcing the population, and governing bodies in particular, to develop alacritous and meaningful memorial responses (1997, 6, 289-91). In considering items left by visitors to the Vietnam Veterans Memorial, Bodnar writes: "a park service technician who helped catalog the items left behind told a reporter that the mementos left him 'a little misty.' He claimed that these objects were 'not like history' but had an 'immediacy' about them. What he might have added was that they were not really like the history that was usually commemorated in public" (1992, 8). Ultimately, Bodnar asserts, "[P]luralism will coexist with hegemony" (253), as civil institutions find it increasingly necessary to accommodate vernacular culture and memory in the formation of public commemorative activities and structures. The roadside cross tradition, not far removed from war memorial customs, similarly spotlights "ordinary" lives and memories, creating polysemic monuments in otherwise banal public space.

In 1993, folklorist George Monger posited two primary reasons for the roadside shrine practice, memorialization, and warning, describing the action of maintaining the site of fatality in such a manner as "private and individual pilgrimage" (114). As a basic motive behind such assemblages, his assertion works well, as a number of my interviewees voiced the same opinion (see chapters four and five). Historian Richard West Sellars and sociologist Tony Walter go further, sensing an almost instinctual need to confront sites of sudden death in an effort to better understand death itself, citing the large crowds that gather for public executions and accidents "simply to observe how other people die" (1993,196). Thus confronting the unknown is a tenet of pilgrimage as conceptualized in the writings of anthropologist Victor Turner (1973, 213-14).

The primary distinction made by Turner with respect to pilgrimage and other rituals is that pilgrimages require a journey (207-8). Such peregrinations are further distinguished by innovation and inclusion, and are thus, as stated by religions scholar Karen Pechilis, "unbounded" (1992, 63). It is this quality of the pilgrimage that creates an environment in which meaning is created and recreated, "an area of multivocality" (Turner and Turner 1978, 145). Moreover, as Pechilis states, "Pilgrimage sites are not the realm of the familiar everyday; therefore the attempt is to make it familiar, to invest it with known meanings. Pilgrimage evokes an application of the known to the unknown in which the known is changed" (65).

The intersection of the familiar and the unfamiliar is commonly marked by, among other things, the action of taking items to or away from the site (66). Thus, the home and the pilgrimage site become invested with the symbols of each. Pilgrims to the Vietnam Veterans Memorial leave teddy bears and articles of clothing and take home a T-shirt or postcard, as those visiting a roadside cross leave a note or figurine and perhaps take away a flower, resulting in a kind of domestication of the site.

Although a site may be familiarized by a variety of actions as a meeting place of different voices and messages, it is also a likely candidate for conflict. For Pechilis and others, the occurrence of discord is not a problematic one. Pilgrimage, as a liminoid phenomenon operating outside of rigid power structures (Turner and Turner 1978, 1-39), provides an open forum for negotiation that does not necessitate resolution (Bowman 1993, 55-56; Pechilis 1992, 65, 71-73). However, there must be some element of agreement at the core of the assemblage. In other words, while the ritual may divert from convention, it must be grounded in established symbolic systems (Pechilis 1992, 67; Hufford 1985, 198).[6]

Religious landscapes, while also reflecting diversity and negotiation, usually mirror religious hegemony. Cultural geographers Terry Jordan and Lester Rowntree note the plethora of crucifixes, crosses, wayside shrines, and Christian place names in Christian, especially Catholic, cultural regions such as Québec and certain parts of Germany. Predominantly Protestant areas, they write, are notable in their relative lack of religious iconography (1990, 219). The sacred landscape of the Austin area bears evidence of the heavy influence of both Catholicism and Protestantism. Its geographic location, in the state as a whole, is important to note here in that it straddles the demographic border between the predominantly Catholic counties to the south and those with heavy Protestant populations to the north (1990, 213; Ramos 1997, 489).

Yi-Fu Tuan emphasizes marginal location as emblematic of anti-structure with reference to Turner's conception of pilgrimage, but also acknowledges the varied character of sacred space, and of the sacred itself (1978, 91, 89). In contrast to the mundane landscape of the modern city, the sacred produces a tension that is awesome, horrible, and yet almost magnetic: "Contemporary space, however colorful and varied, lacks polarized tension as between the numinous and the quotidian. Contemporary life, however pleasant and exciting, moves on one plane—the plane encompassed by rational and humanist vision. Ecstasy and dread, the heights and the depths, the awesome and the transcendent rarely intrude on our lives and on our landscapes except under the influence of chemical stimulus. Along certain lines our world has contracted" (99). While Tuan's statement encompasses the sterility and tedium of the modern suburb and the often tumultuous vibrancy of large cities, it neglects the sacred within the city— the roadside cross, the storefront shrine, the memorial mural.

Anthropologist Alan Morinis identifies pilgrimage sites as "divinely-infused ruptures in the continuous surface of the mundane, human social world" (1984, 281). Though his description is directed to pilgrimage in the Hindu tradition, it is equally applicable to the unexpected and perhaps disruptive nature of impromptu public memorials. In the cultivation of an active connection between site, marker, and memory, they combat more static memorials or what historian Pierre Nora has termed *lieux de mémoire*, "sites of memory". These substitutes for actual "environments of memory," include museum exhibits and festival presentations which "deritualize" (quoted in Kugelmass 1994, 180).

Sites of personal, local, national, and international importance are examples of sacred space, set apart from the quotidian and dedicated to commemoration. In reference to his conception of sanctification, Foote defines sacred spaces as places "that are publicly consecrated or widely venerated rather than those owned or maintained by a particular religious group," further stipulating that "there must be a ceremony that includes an explicit statement of the site's significance and an explanation of why the event should be remembered" (1997, 8). The recognition of roadside cross memorials as sacred space, however, whether temporary or permanent, can occur without formal marking or ceremony. Statements by area residents attest to the extraordinary character of these sites, and their varied roles in the memorialization of people and events.

Religious studies scholar Ian Reader, assessing conventional (e.g., Fatima, the Hajj, Lourdes) and unconventional (e.g., Graceland, Kent State, Dallas' infamous grassy knoll) pilgrimage, concludes, "[P]ilgrimage, in providing a means for uniting the living and the dead, offers the means for individual and social message to be relayed simultaneously without impairing, or bringing into conflict, their separate and multiple meanings" (1993, 21). So, too, roadside memorial markers offer a meeting place for communication, remembrance and reflection, separate from the "everyday." Embracing many voices, they may also represent the quiet acquiescence of civil authority, for in many states their mere existence violates official policy. The multivocality and cooperation embodied in each memorial, and the vernacular support that facilitates their existence, contributes to their dynamism and popularity. The survival of vernacular commemorative tradition, of which roadside crosses are a longstanding and integral part, involves the complex interplay of politics, culture, and belief.

CHAPTER TWO

❧

The Cross-cultural Roadside Cross

In the *Austin American-Statesman* on December 31, 1996, a letter to columnist Jane S. Greig asked, "Where can I get information on the white crosses placed on the highway where someone has died in an accident? I've been told that MADD [Mothers Against Drunk Driving] puts them up where someone has been killed by a drunken driver. I'd like to place a marker at an accident site, but drunken driving was not involved." Greig's response noted that "the only white crosses (markers) legally on the right of way are placed by the Texas Department of Transportation in conjunction with MADD . . . Unauthorized markers periodically appear on the right of way but are removed." The crews assigned to the removal of the markers must have been busy ones, fighting what appeared to be a losing battle. Roadside accident markers, governmentally sanctioned and otherwise, are a familiar feature of many Texas roadways, and indeed of streets and highways across North America.

A folklore discussion list bore this out in a striking fashion. A short query, posted on January 22, 1997, asking "Has anyone come across any articles or books about roadside memorials or accident markers?" soon elicited over fifty responses (Goldstein 1997). Remarkably, while the request was specifically for textual references, many replied not with citations, but with accounts of their own experience. Respondents described roadside cross memorials in nineteen US states—Alabama, California, North and South Carolina, Connecticut, Georgia, Indiana, Kentucky, Massachusetts, Montana, New York, Ohio, Pennsylvania, South Dakota, Tennessee, Utah, Virginia, Washington, and Wyoming, as well as the Canadian province of Newfoundland, Mexico, Panama, England, Germany, Greece, and Ireland. Articles about the roadside cross tradition, or one cross in particular, have appeared in newspapers from Austin to Sydney, Australia (see Banta 1999; Delvecchio 1997).

Popular ideas about roadside memorials are reflected in oral accounts, newspaper and magazine articles which incorporate the memorials in pieces on drunk driving, motor vehicle safety or urban violence, and postcards like that produced by the Center for Southern Folklore depicting a white wooden cross on Highway 82 in Mississippi. Painted in red and black letters, the cross exhorts passing motorists to "GET RIGHT WITH GOD." Web sites devoted to roadside crosses include a journalism student's final project for a "news and new media" class at Northwestern University, and a site originating in Indiana, which offers white crosses for sale (www.netusa1.net/~ghollis/). Another site (no longer operable), which cautioned interested individuals to check local laws concerning roadside memorials prior to making a purchase, offered two alternatives to homemade crosses, stating, "The thought is wonderful but after a very short time the site is not." Florida-based Imago Multimedia memorials featured a dove, in place of overt religious symbolism.

Further evidence of the roadside cross's place in the public imagination exists in popular fiction. From Susan Power's *The Grass Dancer,* "They passed dozens of white crosses along the route, each cross representing a highway fatality. So many Indians smashed themselves on the roads it was old news, but most accidents involved alcohol" (1994, 53). In John Nichols' *The Milagro Beanfield War,* set in small-town New Mexico, an anonymous

Milagro resident protests the plans of wealthy landowner Zopilote Devine by erecting crosses "in memory" of him and his planned development, "Like mushrooms in damp leaves, they sprouted every night by a dozen roadsides—downtown, up in the canyon, out on the north-south highway. Their inscriptions either advised the passerby to *Pray for the soul of Zopilote Devine*, or to *Pray for the dear departed soul of the Miracle Valley Recreation Area*. A few times, even, flowery bouquets had been laid at these contemptible monuments commemorating a death or deaths which had not yet occurred. It was impossible, of course, to ignore the crosses . . . ." (1994, 304). Devine, mortally frightened by the crosses, begins to spend many of his waking hours removing and burning the wooden protests.

Finally, the scene of the tragic bus accident in Russell Banks' *The Sweet Hereafter* is marked, several days afterward, by crosses. Lawyer Mitchell Stevens, inspecting the site, observes, "There had appeared one morning fourteen tiny crosses out at the crash site, which turned out to be the work of schoolchildren, at the instigation of the school board. So much for separation of church and state" (Banks 1991, 138). Banks's novel, set in upstate New York, is based on actual events in the Texas town of Alton, near the Mexican border,[1] including the appearance of the crosses. On the fifth anniversary of the accident in 1994, twenty-one crosses still hung on the chain-link fence around the perimeter of the infamous gravel pit where the bus came to rest after leaving the road (Lemieux 1994). These fictional and factual examples provide a cross-section of the issues that often accompany roadside crosses, such as the separation of church and state, land ownership and reclamation, societal and governmental indifference toward death, and freedom of religious expression.

For instance, a state-sponsored program to memorialize traffic fatalities in Florida with small crosses was abruptly halted when the Department of Transportation and a state representative began to receive complaints about the display of religious symbolism from the local chapter of the Anti-Defamation League. The state had approved the program as a move to curb the increasing construction of roadside crosses by private individuals ("DOT" 1998). The state-constructed crosses already in place were removed and the Department of Transportation later decided to use small disks printed with accident information (Porter 2001). Debate in Halifax, Nova Scotia, about MADD crosses began in January of 1998, with highway officials concerned that they cause motorists undue distraction, and MADD members arguing for increased recognition of impaired driving deaths (Dedrick, Dagle and Dagle 1998). Eventually, MADD crosses were approved for erection along the province's highways.

Thus, the roadside marker landscape is constantly in flux as crosses are erected sometimes within hours of a fatal collision, and others are removed or abandoned. The narratives concerning such crosses are equally mutable, as individuals read about the anniversary of a tragic accident, encounter a cross for the first time upon taking a wrong turn or driving in an area of the city with which they are unfamiliar, or experience a loss themselves.

The underlying beliefs connected to roadside crosses vary as well. In Chile, because an accident victim's spirit is troubled, it remains at the site rather than moving on to the next life. A cross erected at the site is tended not only by friends and family, but by all passersby, who pray to ease the spirit's suffering (Woolf 1996). In El Salvador, the hazards of driving have been incidental to the appearance of memorial crosses. Small villages, devoid of motor vehicles save for small public buses until recently, shared the land with numerous small, white crosses. All death sites were marked with crosses, regardless of the cause. If someone died from a heart attack in a cornfield, a cross was erected there (Escobar 1998).

Wayside calvaries (roadside crucifixion scenes) and crosses line the roads of the Canadian province of Québec (Carpentier 1981), as well as many European countries. Roadside calvaries constructed by West Virginia millionaire Bernard Coffindaffer, consisting of one large cross flanked on either side by two smaller ones are a common sight in twenty-eight states, including Texas. Coffindaffer began erecting the monuments, as instructed by a voice he heard while in the hospital, following his successful recovery from open-heart surgery (see www.christiancrosses.org/). Steve Thomas, an engineer living in the Texas Panhandle town of Pampa, erected a 190-foot cross next to Interstate 40 as an "advertisement for Jesus" in 1995. Thomas planned to help others build giant crosses in Illinois and Florida (Babineck 1997).

Folklorist James Griffith describes three white wooden crosses erected on a hilltop by a friend prior to moving to a new neighborhood in the Pimería Alta region of Arizona. "They stayed up for about five years, until some neighborhood kids dismantled them and took the pieces down the hill. The purpose of the crosses seems to have been protective: they appear to have been intended to make the area a better place in which to live" (1992, 142-43). Similar clusters of crosses, fashioned of wood and sometimes painted, mark a number of hilltops in the area.

Various cross memorials stand throughout England, dating from 1290 to the present. Beginning in the thirteenth century in Britain, crosses were cut into roadside turf in order to purge an accident or crime scene, albeit marking it more permanently than it might have been otherwise. Connecting the custom with that of the formal funeral procession was the practice of pausing along the route to the burial ground for "refreshment, prayers or singing" (Richardson 1993, 96). In Wales, prayers were said at every intersection, while in the Scottish Highlands, mourners added stones to cairns at each stop. Leaving a stone as a sign of remembrance has corollaries in Jewish tradition (Safanov 1948, 78), and in the piles of stones left at a number of the memorials detailed in chapter three. Widely known in southern England are the Eleanor Crosses, marking the resting places of Queen Eleanor's funeral procession on its journey, in 1290, from Lincoln to Westminster Abbey in London. Of the twelve originally erected, only a few remain, including the Victorian reconstruction in London now known as "Charing Cross" (Richardson 1993, 97; Benson 1976, 83-84).

Suicides were commonly buried at crossroads, in an effort to prevent them from becoming revenants (Barber 1988, 30, 55; Taylor 2000, 77). Others have noted that early custom required that anyone considered unworthy of burial in consecrated ground, or at risk of returning to trouble the living, be buried at a cross-roads outside of town, often at the foot of a wayside cross (Benson 1976, 143; Taylor 2000, 77).

By contrast, in Greece memorials known as *proskynetári* may also indicate an individual's escape from death, in which case they are constructed in part to thank divine forces that may have intervened. Like their counterparts that mark a death site, they serve as warnings to motorists and reminders of humans' universal fate (Panourgiá 1995, 172-73). Further, although *proskynetári* often incorporate the cross, they are more usually designed to resemble both churches and gravesites. Anthropologist Neni Panourgiá writes, "they are not large—usually measuring fifty by fifty centimeters—they are set up on pedestals, and instead of walls, they have pieces of glass, like windows. Inside are placed an icon of the particular saint, Christ or Panayia (according to whomever is thought to have intervened), sometimes a photograph of the deceased, a *kandêli* [candle], and a bottle of oil, some charcoal, incense, and matches" (174). As a sign of the frequent and unavoidable intrusion of death into life, the shrines also communicate the desire to prevent accidental death.

Roadside crosses in the American south and southwest are perhaps the most well-documented in the United States, and are often connected with discussions of deathways in Native and Mexican-American traditions (Barerra 1991; Griffith 1992; Owens 1998; McRee and Larcombe 1993; Zimmerman 1997). For example, in the roadside memorialization practice of the Tohono O'odham Indians in southern Arizona, such assemblages represent a combination of O'odham and Catholic belief and date back to a 1958 automobile collision in which seven people were killed. Memorials are constructed only for those who die suddenly, and therefore badly. Distinguishing them from other shrines and aboriginal trail markers on the reservation, the assemblages feature a cross as the primary element while still exhibiting a high degree of individual creativity. Secondary elements may include candles, flowers, fences, saint figurines, and American flags. Although they may be visited and attended to at any time, All Souls Day, November 2, is particularly important in the maintenance cycle. During the week prior and a few days after, the sites are cleaned and redecorated, and prayers are offered for the deceased (Kozak and Lopez 1991).

Until about 1960, the Arizona Highway Department erected similar markers at the sites of fatal accidents. Roadside memorials in Arizona do not always incorporate a cross, however, nor do they commemorate a traffic fatality. For instance, Griffith describes a six-foot-high *nicho* on Interstate 19, "It is made of local stones and whitewashed. Although it is dedicated to Santa Teresa, several statues of other saints and members of the Holy Family share her space. It was erected in memory of Arthur Lee, a former owner of the Sopori Ranch, who fell off his horse in 1934 and was dragged to death. The shrine is traditionally cared for by children at the ranch. The last time I visited it, the space in front of the tiny altar was crowded with candles and artificial flowers" (1992, 104). Although its center point is a *nicho* rather than a cross, the memorial includes items commonly associated with roadside crosses: flowers, candles, stones, and religious icons.

Roadside crosses in Arizona and New Mexico are sometimes assembled from pieces of wreckage, or else constructed of wood, iron, cement, or stone. New Mexico writer Estevan Arrellano's first memory of *descansos* dates from his childhood, "I remember my aunts asking, 'Is your *tío* [uncle] Julian's *descanso* still up?' My *tío* Julian had died at any early age bringing firewood from atop the mesa on a *carro de bestia*, a horse-drawn wagon. To this day, every time I climb the mesa I go directly to his *descanso* and straighten it up with rocks." (1986, 42). Crosses in New Mexico appear in both rural and urban contexts, including Santa Fe street corners (Arellano 1986).

Crosses commemorate deaths both in and outside of cemeteries, and also mark sites of death not caused by automobile accidents. A shrine in a Tijuana, Baja California cemetery was erected at the death and burial site of murdered Mexican soldier Juan Castillo Morales, more commonly called Juan Soldado.[2] Near Waco, Texas, at the former site of the Branch Davidian compound, wooden crosses commemorated those killed during the siege and fire of 1993, until more permanent memorials could be put in place.

The Sign of the Cross

As largely unauthorized markers of liminal space (Graham 1996, 478), roadside crosses, especially on heavily-trafficked urban streets, are dynamic, polysemic communicators. I refer to Charles Peirce's trichotomy of signs to analyze the crosses and their place in Austin's cultural landscape semiotically, specifically his classification of a sign based on the relation between sign and referent. In this regard, roadside crosses fall into all three classes — icon (resemblance), index (contiguity) and symbol (arbitrary relation) (Fiske 1982, 49-57; Nöth 1995, 42-45). As an icon, the cross is "motivated" by the structure, according to Christian tradition, upon which Jesus Christ was crucified. The cross is related indexically to an accident which occurred in a given spot, perhaps the only indication that anything out of the ordinary ever took place there. Symbolically, the cross represents physical death followed by spiritual rebirth into an eternal state of existence to all those even vaguely familiar with the tenets of Christianity. Thus, each marker affords the viewer a powerfully iconic moment, with spatial, temporal, and magico-religious implications.

The cross as an indication of death is connected with the biblical account of Jesus Christ's death and resurrection as told in the gospels of Matthew, Mark, Luke, and John. Prior to the infamous execution, crosses were understood as threatening symbols of Roman power and punishment (Benson 1976, 24). The cross carried extremely negative associations, then, not only for Christians, but for Jews and other groups alike who had suffered under Roman rule (Henry 1925, 23; Rees 1992, 69). As such, the cross was a symbol of brutal death, and thus rejected for use in worship by the early Christians until late in the fourth century, and then not bearing any representation of Christ.[3] The crucifix, a cross with the figure of Christ upon it, entered into regular use in the eighth century (Firth 1973, 48). The beginning of the cross's acceptance as a religious symbol may be found in the writings of Saint Paul to the Galatians (Henry 1925, 23-24). Paul rejected the world as he felt Christians were then rejected by Roman society, "But God forbid that I should glory, save in the cross of our Lord Jesus Christ, by whom the world is crucified unto me, and I unto the world" (Gal. 6: 14).

The cross is also connected with the idea of the "cosmic world tree," representing the continuity of the life cycle (Rees 1992, 69-70; see also McDannell 1995, 120-121). Other associations with the tree, and thus immortality, result from the embrace of both good and evil by the crucifixion. "The tree of the knowledge of good and evil in Eden is replaced by the trees on which the good and evil thieves are crucified. The crucifixion of Jesus represents the absorption of the other side of things into a complete whole: Jesus accepts both the good thief and the bad . . . ." (Reese 98). Theologian Gustaf Aulén also stresses the cross's symbolic duality while insisting on its singular conclusion. Indeed, the "gospel of the cross" preached by the apostles depended upon the death *and* resurrection of Jesus Christ (1970, 188). Further, in the actual and symbolic suffering of Christ, he is experientially connected to all of humankind (169; Tuan 1978, 98), and made the perfect instrument of reconciliation: "And having made peace through the blood of his cross, by him to reconcile all things unto himself; by him I say, whether they be things in earth, or things in heaven" (Col. 1:20). In the horror of the crucifixion, Aulén emphasizes the link between the harsh reality of human existence, including "human wickedness and hardness, . . . accidents, catastrophes," the suffering of Christ and thus of God (1970, 186, 167); however, it is equally important to recognize, in this tribulation, the victory represented by Christ's empty tomb, which in turn is symbolized by the "empty" cross.

The acceptance of both good and evil, and the final triumph of good through eternal life, is crucial to many of my informants' understanding not only of the loss of their loved ones, but of the message of the roadside crosses. Some stressed that visiting their childrens' grave sites, while important to them, is tempered by the knowledge that their children are not there. Further, while some are convinced of their children's presence at the respective accident sites, they also believe them to be in heaven. Indeed, religious expression, while reinforcing perceived links between humankind and Jesus Christ, by no means fixes him to a certain place or time. As the risen Christ, "the promise of his presence is every day to the end of time" (Aulén 1970, 182). Thus, just as the physical and verbal symbolism related to Christ does not anchor him in the space-time continuum, neither are the accident victims magico-religiously affixed to their death sites by means of the cross.

Powerful symbolism aside, the cross may be viewed with some suspicion by Protestant groups in the southern United States, who regard it as more indicative of Catholicism than a pan-Christian emblem (Jordan 1982, 50-51). The sentiment was echoed in my interview with Shilah Lamay, during which she discussed her ambivalence toward the cross erected in memory of her daughter Heather by schoolmates. Moreover, utilizing Christian symbolism to make a political statement, as in the case of Mothers Against Drunk Driving memorials, is a tradition in American public life that seemingly contradicts the legal separation of church and state. It is, however, in keeping with the concept of civil religion, first expounded by Jean Jacques Rousseau in *The Social Contract*.

Sociologist Robert Bellah has written extensively on the idea of American civil religion, from an examination of the Declaration of Independence to the rhetoric of the Johnson administration (1963-69), noting a common "set of beliefs, symbols, and rituals" (1990, 62) e.g., a belief in "the Almighty," the cross, and the observance of Memorial Day. Of relevance to the present discussion is his differentiation between denominationally defined faiths such as Catholicism, Protestantism, and Judaism, and the "very activist and noncontemplative conception of the fundamental religious obligation" (264). As civil religion is not typified by the hushed seclusion of a cathedral, chapel or temple, but thoroughly grounded in the activity of the public arena, denominational differences are obscured.[4]

Civil religion is invoked, especially, in times of crisis and uncertainty, as during the war between the states, the assassination of President Kennedy, the Vietnam war, the ongoing AIDS crisis, and the terror attacks in New York City and Washington, D.C. Indeed, in 1995, literature and religious studies scholar Peter S. Hawkins cited "the acts of piety that have grown up around both the VVM [Vietnam Veterans Memorial] and the [AIDS] quilt" as "the most vital examples of popular civil religion we have" (1995, 762). At public sites where the sacred and profane intermingle, people of varying cultural, and thus religious, backgrounds come together to mourn.

In theory, civil religion's all-encompassing public embrace excludes religious intolerance, with an emphasis on Christian symbolism without specific invocation of the Christian church (Bellah 1990, 264, 267), similar to the use of the cross without strict adherence to the beliefs in which its religious significance originated. Hence, it becomes representative of religious or spiritual belief in general, a symbol adoptable by diverse individuals and groups.

Crosses, Custom and Civil Religion

Texas was not officially part of the United States until the sign-ing of the Treaty of Guadalupe Hidalgo in 1848 (Fehrenbach 2000, 272-273). The Austin area was the northernmost point of a number of Spanish expeditions and a few failed missions, but the more successful settlements date from the period of Mexican rule. Present-day Bastrop, for example, southeast of Austin on Highway 71, is the result of an 1832 Mexican land grant. How-ever, the present Mexican-American population in the region may be more directly connected with recent immigration, rather than early colonization (Simons and Hoyt 1992, 177-78). At any rate, cultural ties to border areas remain strong. Often, immigrants in the Austin area are also helping to support relatives in Mexico.

Mexican culture is a part of everyday life for many individuals in central Texas, in street (e.g., Guadalupe, Nueces, and Rio Grande streets) and place names (Mendez Junior High School and Américo Paredes Elementary School). Further evidence comes in the form of: a regional dialect that incorporates countless Spanish words and expressions; Tex-Mex, the regional cuisine; Tejano music; holiday celebrations on *Diez y Seis, Cinco de Mayo,* and *el Dia de los Muertos;* and customs, such as birthday *piñatas* and roadside crosses.

Early Catholic priests and settlers brought with them death customs including that of burying fellow believers in hallowed ground, or *camposanto.* In the early days of Spanish colonization of the Americas, when travelers often found themselves far be-tween established settlements, those dying en route had to be buried *in situ.* Crosses at the site of interment served not only to mark the spot, but to informally consecrate it (Barrera 1991, 278).

Historical references to the custom of marking significant sites, including graves, with a cross include those found in correspon-dence and journals dating from the time of Spanish exploration of the area, prior to settlement. The diary entries of Fernando del Bosque, on a journey across the Rio Grande toward present-day

Eagle Pass and perhaps beyond in 1675, record the numerous instances in which a wooden cross was constructed and erected to claim land for the Spanish monarch ([1908] 1963, 293-307), as do those of Juan Domínguez de Mendoza, on a 1684 expedition to western central Texas ([1908] 1963, 321-333). Alonso de León (son of Ponce de León) made five expeditions into Texas, the first in 1686 and the last in 1690. It was during the last foray that he recorded, "As we went down toward the river [Rio Hondo] we found some large white rocks, on some of which we saw some crosses cut, and other figures artificially made with great skill, apparently a long time before" ([1908] 1963, 392).

Descansos (resting places) were erected in Embudo, New Mexico at least as far back as the 1700s, during which time they were banned by the governor: "There were so many that travelers who stopped to pray for the souls of the departed became easy targets for the Indians. . ." (Arrellano 1986, 42). Griffith cites a Franciscan historian's translation of the complaint of a Catholic bishop, circa 1783, about "the large number of crosses on a road where travelers were being killed by Apache Indians" (Woolf 1996; Griffith 1992, 101-102).[5]

Jean Louis Berlandier describes a trip made in August of 1829 from Laredo to Matamoros, during which he and his fellow travellers encountered more than thirty crosses. Initially, they thought the crosses were indicative of recent deaths at the hands of bandits. But, "[L]ater we learned that several crosses were very old and indicated places where the Comanches had massacred travellers or herdsmen. Lastly, we learned that rancheros sometimes bury their relatives in these places, or else put a cross at the spot where they rest with a corpse which they are taking for burial to the cemetery of a neighboring town" (1980, 429).

At the same time, other burials were similarly marked. In 1828, Berlandier and his party, passing through recent battlesites of Mexico's war of independence, saw soldiers' remains everywhere, as the dead were sometimes left as they fell. It is in this context that he notes the contrasting humanity of Colonel José Félix Trespalacios (on the Mexican side): "He gave burial to almost all the dead which were found. At the foot of an old oak, respected by the years, a grave was dug, and the remains of those adventurers who arrived to proclaim independence were buried. A cross carved in the trunk of that live oak indicated the site of the grave. Placed at the height of a man's head, renewed from time to time by the soldiers of the presidio who carve it as deep as the wood, it seems to be freshly engraved" (284). Not all accidental or military deaths were consecrated in such a manner, however. Berlandier documents their discovery of at least one corpse that they happened upon and apparently left to decompose (233).

Father Damían Massanet, who accompanied Alonso de León on two sojourns into Texas, notes a similar occurrence, in which Indians led him to a spot where the dead bodies of two Frenchmen lay ([1908] 1963, 391). However, De León's account of the same incident is quite different. He writes, "we came to where they told us two Frenchmen had died, where they wished to make a settlement, and where we saw the graves. We placed a cross in a tree for them . . ."(417). The discrepancy between the two accounts underscores the difficulty of tracking the appearance and disappearance of roadside crosses. Arrellano, seeking out an 1846 Taos Rebellion battle site along the Old Apodaca Trail—he had read about it while researching his family's genealogy in an old journal—came upon rocks literally covered with crosses (1986, 42). Like many items of folklore, *descansos* have often been deemed superfluous to the historical record, except when problematic as in the case of Griffith's Catholic bishop or Embudo's eighteenth-century governor.

In accordance with Berlandier's account, folklorist John O. West identifies the custom with the transport of the coffin from the church to the *camposanto* following a funeral. The places at which the pallbearers stopped to rest were *descansos*, as were the places of ritual pausing—to recite the rosary or a requiem prayer—

inside the cemetery. Older cemeteries featured *descanso* shelters. Thus, the *descansos* represented a very real, as well as metaphorical, interruption of life's journey, as do roadside crosses today (1988, 236-39).

Many Mexican-Americans view the tradition as a distinctly Mexican one adopted by "Anglos." Although in north and central America the crosses are fashioned out of many different materials, including wood, metal, cement, and sometimes pieces of the wrecked automobile(s). That most commonly occurring in Texas, as in Mexico, is the white, wooden cross, usually accompanied by flowers, and perhaps other items such as photographs, notes, and/or religious objects.

In the recent past, policy decisions regarding roadside crosses were made at the discretion of each of the Texas Department of Transportation's (TxDoT) twenty-five district enforcement agencies. The city of Austin and the surrounding area comprises the "Austin district." Some agencies chose to allow the erection and maintenance of certain types of markers, such as those constructed by Mothers Against Drunk Driving,[6] while others adopted a strict no-marker stance, such as the Dallas district. MADD memorials were the only authorized roadside markers in the Austin district until November 2001, when TXDoT policy was amended to allow markers to be erected for any traffic fatality through department offices.

The Austin MADD chapter, known as the Heart of Texas Chapter, maintains records of crosses erected through the organization, and the Austin TxDoT enforcement agency keeps a file of MADD cross "permits" (Ohlendorf 1997).[7] To erect a cross through the Heart of Texas MADD Chapter, individuals must complete a form available through the chapter office that includes construction specifications and guidelines. Following submission of the application, an organization representative files a similar form with the TxDoT. The form stipulates that the District Engineer reserves the right to remove the cross if it is deemed to be hazardous to drivers in any way.

Texas residents have erected roadside crosses in all regions of the state. South Texas's increasing proliferation of crosses, in fact, has been problematic for TxDoT officials. In the spring of 1997, an engineer in the Austin district office made a special presentation to a group of highway maintenance supervisors on the roadside cross "problem" in the Valley, specifically the Pharr district (encompassing Brooks, Cameron, Hidalgo, Jim Hogg, Kenedy, Starr, Willacy, and Zapata counties). The assemblages had become so numerous as to render routine roadway maintenance difficult. Additionally, TxDoT officials feared they were dangerously distracting to drivers (Hurt 1997). Folklorist Alberto Barrera documented over forty-eight crosses in Starr County alone at the beginning of the 1990s (1991, 292). The southern county, at the edge of the Texas-Mexican border, is home to approximately 49,000 people and is one of the fastest growing counties in the state (Ramos 1997, 268). In keeping with popular belief about roadside crosses in the state, the population of Starr county is primarily Hispanic (97.2%), and Roman Catholic (85.6%).

As Barrera found in his sample, however, it is important to note that not all Mexican-American Catholics practice the custom (279). Indeed, the custom is quite widespread outside its community of origin. Counties with considerably smaller Hispanic and Catholic populations are also home to similarly styled roadside memorial assemblages, such as Blanco, Gillespie, and Kerr counties, to the west of the Austin area (Ramos 1997, 152, 195, 222, 488-89).

As well, south central Texas is home to a number of historic German settlements. Galveston, San Antonio, and Houston had considerable German populations by the end of the 1800s, between one-quarter and one-third of the total (Jordan, Bean, and Holmes 1984, 85-86). The German, and largely Lutheran, heritage of these areas, especially historic German settlements such as Fredericksburg in Gillespie county, still marks the landscape, examples of which are the material and form of the area's roadside crosses (Jordan 1982, 105-15). I photographed seven in between Johnson City and Kerrville, travelling by U. S. Highway 290 west and State Highway 16.

Set back from the road against a barbed wire fence running alongside State Highway 16 between Kerrville and Fredericksburg is a sheet metal cross, painted white, for Tori Eckhardt (Fig. 2.1). The cross stands about six feet high, and features a photo-ceramic portrait of Tori at its center. A small black plaque with gold lettering, a few inches below the photo on the vertical, reads:

IN MEMORY
OF
TORI
ECKHARDT
10-11-77 — 9-26-95

Further down the vertical is a large red bow and an arrangement of red poinsettias. Just south of the cross, a visitor has placed a large Christmas wreath supported by a wire stand.

A similarly constructed cross, also fashioned from white sheet metal, stands several yards from US 290 at the rear of a highway rest stop. Approximately a foot shorter than the cross described above, its intricate design includes an almost identical plaque as well as an attached plant holder. The plaque states:

IN LOVING
MEMORY OF
OUR BELOVED
KRISTA
MAE
VOLLMAR
8-27-72—6-9-91

Fig. 2.1 Sheet metal cross for Tori Eckhardt on Highway 16

Flanking the cross on its eastern side, a two-foot limestone cross stands in front of three large stones. The cross's face is inscribed with countless "X"s, or Saint Andrew's crosses, the significance of which is unknown (Fig. 2.2).[8]

Crosses also intermittently appear alongside US 290 heading east out of Austin, varying in size, construction, and decoration. Many are without identifying markings or inscriptions, whether by design or age. Farm to Market Road 1488 intersects 290 in the town of Hempstead. I photographed two memorials on the two-lane highway, including one consisting of a Calvary-like display of three crosses set back a few yards from the road. The tallest of the white, wooden crosses, approximately two and a half feet high, is flanked on either side by the two others of almost equal height. The large grapevine wreath to the east of the crosses, featuring pink silk roses, greenery, and a card of condolence firmly links the assemblage to traffic fatalities.[9]

Another roadside cross, unique to the sample area, stands roughly thirty miles east of the three crosses noted above on the same highway (Fig. 2.3). The memorial features an eighteen-inch cross atop a wooden picket fence, almost identical to the *cerquitas* (little fences) serving as grave site boundaries in many Mexican-American cemeteries in Texas and New Mexico (Jordan 1982, 70-71). The entire structure is painted white. The side of the *cerquita* parallel to the roadway has been decorated with a lasso and three or four bouquets of artificial flowers. At the time I photographed the memorial, there was no evidence of anything inside the boundary of the fence.

The population in the counties through which these sections of US 290 and FM 1488 run, with the exception of Travis county, is predominately white, Euro-North American, with African Americans comprising the next largest group in all but Montgomery county (Ramos, 1997, 148, 189, 228, 243, 282-83). In Montgomery county, in which the above cross and *cerquita* stand, Hispanics comprise the second largest demographic group. Additionally, the area presents a mix of dominant religious groups, including Southern Baptist, Roman Catholic, and Lutheran.

During the course of a half-hour drive from Conroe, the largest city in Montgomery County, to New Caney, I photographed ten crosses. In contrast to those documented on 290 and 1488, all but one of the ten bear at least a name, if nothing else. Three metal crosses, painted white with black lettering, were each attended by white, red, and purple silk poinsettias driven into the ground at the base. It is important to note that the crosses are not grouped together, indicating that each spot is significant and likely an actual death site. The cross farthest from the road is the most explicit in this regard (Fig. 2.4), and reads:

INRI
AQUI FALLECIO
ALBERTO FUGAROS
RECUEDOS [sic]
DE ESPOSA E HIJA Y FAM.
DECANSA EN PAZ
8-4-68—21-7-95
[Here died/Alberto Fugaros
remembrance from wife and daughter and family
rest in peace].

Nearer the road are the crosses for Antonio Hernandez Bolanos ("RECUERDO DE FAM Y AMIGOS, FALLECIO 21-7-95") and Lazaro Hernandez Zamudio ("RECUERDO DE FAM Y AMIGOS, NACIO EL 2/4/76, FALLECIO EL 21/7/95"). The crosses are among the more traditional memorials included in this study, in terms of their construction, spatial arrangement, and Spanish epitaphs. Further east, the memorial for Jerry Lee Adams, resting in a bed of clover, combines a white wooden cross with a planter base. Tributes include artificial flowers and a package of M&M candy.

Fig. 2.2 Limestone cross with inscribed "X"s

Fig. 2.3 Cross and *cerquita* on 1488 near Interstate 45

This short sampling of crosses outside the main study area, together with those documented by Barrera, provides a useful cross-section of vernacular roadside memorials in the state and highlights the variety of construction and design that marks the custom. Like the counties upon which I focus in the following chapters, Travis and Hays, those described above straddle cultural borders, namely Catholic and Protestant, and Euro-North American and Mexican-American.

The influence of Catholic, hispanic culture is certainly strong in the area, permeating central Texans' day-to-day existence. Consequently, a custom such as that of the roadside cross, with roots in Spanish tradition, may be practiced by a Southern Baptist female of British descent with little concern for its origin or similarity to other of her beliefs. Additionally, the tradition has variants in a number of cultures, as detailed above, and is a feature of popular culture as well.

The symbolic strength of the cross derives from centuries of association with powerful images of suffering and hope. It continues to be informed by the controversy its presentation invariably evokes. In contrast to the plethora of official historical markers and monuments in the Austin area, handcrafted and often meticulously maintained roadside memorials communicate more personally about events in the present, rather than the past. The Austin area's roadside crosses represent individual and community responses to the grief, anger, frustration, and anxiety about vehicular carelessness and crime, and the dangers of urban space.

Fig. 2.4 Cross farthest from road, for Alberto Fugaros

CHAPTER THREE

༄

Roadside Memorial
Case Studies

As Austin's population and urban sprawl increases, more and more people find themselves commuting to jobs in the city, with as much as three hours a day spent in transit. Oftentimes their daily drive takes them past at least one roadside memorial. Between April 1997 and January 1998, I documented thirty-five memorial sites in and around Austin (Fig. 3.1). A number of these memorials have already been dismantled or significantly altered while new ones have been constructed.

As noted in the previous chapter, MADD markers, such as the crosses pictured here, have until very recently been the only roadside memorials approved for the Austin district by the Texas Department of Transportation. Jennifer Solter founded one of the first MADD chapters in Texas, the Heart of Texas Chapter, following the death of her daughter Sara Jayne Solter in 1981. In the early-to-mid-1980s, all MADD crosses in Texas were built by a Houston resident who had lost a son to a drunk driving incident. Solter erected one of these white crosses in 1984, under the canopy of a poplar tree at the edge of a residential area.

The red plaque at the crosspiece reads:

IN LOVING MEMORY OF SARA JAYNE SOLTER
BORN 10/20/61 & KILLED AT
THIS LOCATION 8/14/81 BY A DRUNK DRIVER

Friends and family place artificial flowers at the base of the cross in conjunction with Sara's birthday, Christmas, and Easter (Fig. 3.2). Jennifer stated that, "Those are the three times that we always change out the flowers for." The red tulips pictured here were left for Easter. Sometimes she finds items left anonymously, such as a rose with a red ribbon tied around it, or dried or artificial flowers.

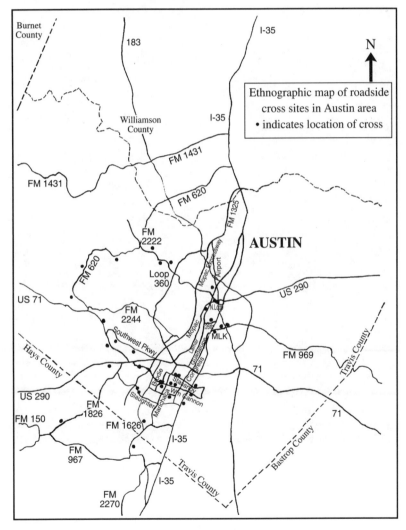

Fig. 3.1 Memorial sites in Austin area

Fig. 3.2 First MADD cross in Austin,
erected in memory of Sara Jayne Solter

The front lawn of the nearby Dittmar Recreation Center, just over a mile to the southeast of Solter's memorial, is the site of a MADD cross erected for Theresa Lynn Ellsworth Moore, killed a week after her thirty-fourth birthday. The incident occurred at the intersection of Dittmar and Forest Woods Roads, an area known by residents for poor visibility and speeding motorists. The cross is difficult to see as it stands parallel to the road. Conforming to MADD standards, the cross is inscribed thus:

IN LOVING MEMORY OF
THERESA LYNN ELLSWORTH MOORE
BORN JULY 14, 1960 & KILLED AT
THIS LOCATION JULY 21, 1994 BY
A DRUNK DRIVER

Moore was fatally injured when her vehicle was struck from behind as she exited the recreation center parking lot. Although no flowers or other decorative items were in evidence at the memorial when I photographed it in January of 1998, an electrical pole across the street was adorned with a tattered pinwheel and plastic flowers. Pink plastic roses were attached to the base of the pole.

Farm to Market Road 2222 is well-known throughout Austin as an extremely dangerous roadway. It is also a popular one, for it runs from northwest Austin to a number of city and county park areas bordering lakes with sandy beaches.[1] A weather-worn MADD cross sits high on a newly-constructed ridge on the north side of the road just at the city limit. Over a decade old, the fading plaque nailed to the flaking, white cross still bears the inscription:

IN LOVING MEMORY OF
ROBERT CARTER MANLY
D.O.B. 1/10/66
KILLED ON THIS SPOT BY A DRUNK DRIVER
5/21/85

Fig. 3.3 Northernmost memorial for Daniel London and Beth Early

In May of 1997, two desiccated wildflowers were secured to the top of the transverse beam with a smooth, round chalk rock.

Two crosses not constructed through MADD memorializing a drunk-driving incident bear the first names of both victims, Daniel London and Beth Early. Daniel was driving Beth home from a date when their vehicle was struck head-on by an oncoming vehicle. Located on Brodie Lane, just north of FM 1626, both crosses stand parallel to the road. Several groupings of silk flowers surround the base of each cross. The northernmost, a white, wooden cross stands over white and red poinsettias, red carnations, and purple daisies (Fig. 3.3). A gold-tone angel, held fast with a band of red flowers, adorns the transverse, painted in two-inch, pine-green letters. The cross is also fronted by a plain wooden cross, about eighteen inches high. A pink bow and two pink silk carnations backed by greenery form a diagonal across its face.

Daniel's mother, Ana Garcia, erected the wrought-iron cross handmade in her home state of Jalisco, Mexico (Harmon 1997). Anchored in concrete and painted white, Daniel and Beth's names, in capital letters fashioned of clay, are separated by a five-petal flower of the same material (Fig. 3.4). The planter attached to the cross holds three clay pots filled with a profusion of flowers, among them daisies, black-eyed Susans, morning glories, and daffodils. Set back a couple of yards from the road, the crosses are obscured by the sharp curve of the road, and the high grass on either side of them as one approaches from the north or south.

An unmarked cross on FM 620 also commemorates a drunk driving fatality which occurred sometime after May of 1995 (Biggs 1998). Facing oncoming traffic, the white wooden cross with beveled ends shows signs of wear in the chipped paint and the almost colorless silk flowers deteriorating at its base. A rusted nail and a bit of string are all that is left of something that was once attached near the top of the south face of the memorial. A chunky, red wooden heart pendant hangs from the cross piece by a thin leather strip.

Another memorial not visibly connected to MADD has been

Fig. 3.4 Wrought-iron cross and planter handmade in Jalisco, Mexico

constructed on a median of West William Cannon Boulevard for former Houston resident and drunk driving victim Mark Travis Phillips. About two feet in length, the letters "M" and "P" spelled out in rocks decorate the ground in front of an eighteen-inch cross, fashioned of thin metal and painted white, held in place by a small pile of stones. A broken terra-cotta planter, still holding two dried stems, sits above the second point of the "M." The *Austin American-Statesman* reported on February 26, 1996 that the driver, charged with intoxication manslaughter, had either fallen asleep or passed out at the wheel. Phillips, age twenty-two, was killed when the car in which he was a passenger skipped the curb of the median and slammed into a tree. Now part of the memorial, the scarred tree is ringed by stones. Inside the ring is debris from the wreck and a single, empty beer bottle.

Conjecture and Certainty, Curves and Collisions

Unlike Phillips' memorial, those for which no additional information can be found pose an ethnographic problem—the cause of the signified accident cannot be ascertained with certainty. However, as part of Texas' Hill Country, Austin and the surrounding area is rife with scenic, and treacherous roads that link urban congestion with glistening lakes and rolling hills. The views afforded a traveler are distracting enough in the best of conditions. A number of roadside crosses in the area informally mark blind or sudden curves, and often lie within several yards of an official highway warning sign.

State Highway 71 merges with United States Highway 290 as both intersect Interstate Highway 35 in the middle of the city, and the two roads run together for eight and a half miles to the west, separating again at the "Y" in Oak Hill. Just outside the city limit on US 290 is perhaps the oldest extant cross in the metropolitan area, measuring one and one-half by two feet (Fig. 3.5). Well-weathered and peeling, the white, wooden cross overlooks two lanes of oncoming traffic at a ninety degree angle from atop a small hill.

Fig. 3.5 Cross, possibly dating from 1970s, on Highway 71 west

Fig. 3.6 Looking toward Highway 71 west, cross with grapevine wreath facing westbound lanes

Pink and white plastic rose blossoms flank the cross on one side, and a rusted license plate lies face down in front of it. Turning the plate over, the words "Texas Truck" and the year "'72" are legible.

Highway 71 west, as it moves north of 290's course, winds its way through some of central Texas' more spectacular vistas. West of Austin, a white wooden cross halfway up the hillside bore a grapevine wreath, with a colorful array of flowers, greenery, and a large, white and blue patterned bow (Fig. 3.6). The wreath hung from the vertical piece, and from the transverse, secured with faded pink ribbon, was a sprig of six sunflowers. Closer inspection revealed car parts among the flowers at the base of the memorial. A windshield wiper, pieces of brake and turn signal lights, a radiator cap, and bits of tire and black plastic were scattered among rocks placed at a forty-five degree angle with the base of the cross.

Further toward Austin on the same highway, about twelve miles outside city limits, was one of the most elaborate memorials in the area. The two by three feet, white, wooden cross, simply constructed, was just one part of the large assemblage parallel to the four-lane, undivided highway. Hanging from it were three wreaths: a large Christmas wreath, approximately two feet in diameter, decorated with bows and ornaments; a ceramic Easter wreath (incorporating pastel-colored rabbits, flowers and birds); and hanging on the back side of the cross, a grapevine wreath upon which sat a ceramic angel (Fig. 3.7). Two rosaries dangled from the crosspiece, almost touching the angel's face. Below the angel, on the ground, was a grouping of unidentifiable car parts.

The cross was topped with a gold-tone angel vase containing a silk lily. Two bunches of these lilies flanked the base of the cross. Large pink lilies sat beside a stuffed gorilla, and a line of single bluebonnets formed a soft front border ending with a bunch of poinsettias. In between these and one cluster of lilies lay a baseball cap, secured in the back with a rock, emblazoned with the Ford logo and the words "Bad Ass Boys With Bad Ass Toys." Bordering the entire assemblage was a heart-shaped border of large, flat rocks.

Fig. 3.7 Memorial viewed from front, at edge of stone circle

Austin photographer Doug Powell has taken several pictures of the memorial. He told me that a few years ago, visitors used a magic marker left at the site to write messages to the accident victim on the cross. The marker was no longer there when I visited the site, and the missives had either been erased by exposure to the elements or a fresh coat of paint. Time, as well as the effects of sun, wind, and rain, take their toll on all memorials.

Roughly one-half mile west of the memorial, Southwest Parkway dead-ends into Highway 71. One mile east of the intersection is the white, wrought-iron cross bearing the name Kevin Attison. The name runs down the vertical of the structure, and the horizontal gives his dates of birth ("2-7-67") and death ("7-18-89"), all in white clay figures. A wreath of faded silk flowers, red carnations, white impatiens, and greenery is affixed to the transverse with a length of rusting wire. Two bunches of similarly weathered silk roses lie horizontally about the base, along with a single carnation bloom.

Fig. 3.8 Newly-erected cross, adorned with floral spray and lapel pin, on FM 2222

Just west of Austin city limits on FM 2222, I photographed a cross that appeared to be newly constructed. A diagonal spray of yellow silk roses and greenery adorned a white styrofoam cross, to which had also been attached a lapel pin promoting a local restaurant (Fig. 3.8). Attached by a layer of white gauze tape to a thin length of unfinished wood, the structure was further supported by pieces of barrier support beams likely dislodged in the crash. The assemblage was fronted by the dented metal guard rail, sprayed red to indicate the need for repair work.

Back in the city proper, motorists travelling east on North Loop Boulevard between Guadalupe Street and Airport Boulevard encounter a blind curve just prior to an intersection populated by several small businesses. If concentrating on the road, they may not notice the four wooden crosses of various dimensions and finishes that border the fence line of a small state cemetery. The westernmost of the four, standing alone between two tall bushes, is neither painted nor decorated save for a rusted car part resting on the top of the vertical piece. Also constructed of unfinished wood is the easternmost cross, bearing no decoration or identifying marks. Nearer the other two crosses, it has been driven into the ground in front of a fire hydrant. Approximately one-and-a-half yards southwest of it is a similarly constructed cross, its frame attached to the cemetery fence. Faded lettering inscribed in black ink covers the surface of the cross. Still legible is the name "David Crowley" running along the vertical, and the phrases "Born January 16, 1965" and "Asleep in the Lord" across the horizontal. A small white teddy bear, placed between the horizontal and the fence just above the date, serves as decoration along with a ribbon which anchors the cross to the chain-link fence. A rusted piece of wire affixes the vertical.

The largest and most detailed cross of the four also bears Crowley's name. A black and gold-tone plaque with gold lettering at the crosspiece reads:

IN MEMORY OF
DAVID M. CROWLEY
JANUARY 16, 1965 — OCTOBER 16, 1995
"You always have been, and forever will be, my friend."[2]

The cross is finished with a dark wood stain. A plastic Santa Claus ornament hangs from the transverse. Scattered among a number of large rocks supporting the base are a pine cone and two Christmas ornaments, as well as silk flowers and greenery. Threaded through the fence behind the two crosses are a number of items including a purple tassel, a withered bouquet of fresh flowers wrapped in plastic, a laminated photo of a young man in a tuxedo, a string of plastic Easter eggs, ribbons, a bungee cord, and a dreamcatcher[3] protected by a plastic covering (Fig. 3.9).

Although two Austin residents mentioned the site to me, they had no knowledge of what had occurred there. Moreover, I was unable to find any information concerning David Crowley or any accident in the area near the date indicated on the cross.

Equally enigmatic are the crosses erected in memory of Mario Castor, who died on July 9, 1996. Located off IH-35 on Stassney Lane, they border the eastbound lanes passing over Williamson Creek. Attached to the bridge itself, the first is a small, unpainted cross standing just over a foot tall. The deceased's name, along with messages, such as "I LOVE YOU," have been printed with a black felt-tip marker. Other messages have been left on the bridge railing: "GOD LOVES YOU MARIO CASTOR," and "MARIO, MAY YOU REST IN PEACE, LOVE YOU ALWAYS, YOUR AUNT, JANIE CANTU, FRIEND JUAN DOMINGUEZ." Multi-colored ribbons affix funeral sprays to the railing—a wreath of blue silk carnations, greenery, two blue bows, and a lavender ribbon bearing the word "Father" in silver lettering; and a grouping of pink and red silk carnations, daisies, and greenery surrounding a red bow. A single, faded silk poinsettia is fastened to the center of the cross.

Fig. 3.9 Two crosses bearing David Crowley's name and surrounded
by items hung from the chain-link fence

Two yards to the east, at the bridge railing's end, a larger,
white wooden cross sits amid a display of silk flowers including
white and yellow chrysanthemums. Pink and white rose buds,
purple lilies, and white and pink carnations sprout from a white
vase attached to the vertical. At the top of the vertical, a wooden
cut-out in the form of a open book bears the sentence "Thru the
Love of God We feel Eternal Life." The white plastic crucifix at
the center of the cross is backed by a sprig of plastic greenery, and
flanked on either end of the crossbar with wooden dove cut-outs
also painted white. Black lettering on the transverse reads "MARIO
CASTOR, 1963–1996." In August of 1997 a *nicho* holding a
small portrait of the Virgin Mary sat atop the vertical, but was
gone by the following December (Fig. 3.10).

Fig. 3.10 Castor's cross in the summer of 1997
(Photo courtesy of Christie Everett)

A similarly complex memorial commands the attention of west-bound motorists on Slaughter Lane, just east of Austin's Bowie High School (Fig. 3.11). The *Austin-American Statesman* reported that Heather Werchan, a few days shy of eighteen, was one of two passengers in a truck travelling west on Slaughter that veered off the road and crashed into a tree on May 10, 1997. The cross was constructed by the driver of the vehicle, Heather's boyfriend, and another school friend. A few feet to the southwest of the cross, the driver and his mother planted a miniature rose bush (Werchan 1998).

At approximately four-and-one-half feet by four-and-one-half feet, the cross is the largest documented within city limits. As shown, "Heather" is spelled out in large, pine green letters which hang across the horizontal piece. Strands of silk sunflowers, black-eyed Susans, orange marigolds, autumn-colored leaves, and other greenery are intertwined about both pieces of the structure. A stuffed teddy bear, with a plastic-covered photograph of Heather attached with purple ribbon to its right foot, sits on the horizontal near the transverse, along with a ring of purple silk miniature roses. Higher up and around the vertical, a visitor has placed a Bowie graduation tassel (in school colors of red and black). Sitting atop the vertical are five carefully placed pennies—one at each corner, and one in the middle.

The same green letters indicate her middle and last initials on the bottom half of the vertical. A holiday wreath, ornamented by pine cones, holly, miniature musical instruments, and presents,

Fig. 3.11 Memorial for Heather Werchan on Slaughter Lane,
including rose bush and large cross

encircles the "N", for Nicole. The "W" is entirely obscured from view by silk poinsettias in a terra-cotta pot, flanked on one side by an empty flower vase and on the other by red and white silk roses stuck in the ground. A white porcelain angel kneels in prayer in front of the bouquet. Surrounding the assemblage are large, rectangular stones. Lengths of artificial ivy and small stones are scattered about the base, one securing a handwritten note, the words of which had been blurred by rainfall.

FM 1626, at the southern edge of the city, runs parallel to Slaughter Lane for approximately three miles, then turns sharply south toward the Travis County line. The memorial to Armando Carrizales, constructed in front of a barbed wire fence a few yards from the roadway, lies in adjacent Hays County (Fig. 3.12). A piece of barrier support beam is the five foot vertical piece; varnished pressurized wood, decorated with electrical tape, makes the horizontal piece of equal length. Two unfinished wood pieces, forming diagonal supports running from the lower half of the vertical to the crossbar give Carrizales's date of birth, March 10, 1947, and death, October 10, 1995. The numbers, as well as the deceased's name on the crossbar, are a result of careful wood burning.

Ceramic electrical insulators top the vertical and both ends of the transverse, while another is attached to the north side of the vertical nearer the ground. A black bandana encircles the post below the insulator, from which is hung a clear plastic bell. Two wreaths decorate the cross, the first formed of three strands of electrical wiring and lengths of mistletoe. An orange electrical tape bow, a miniature deer, and a pine cone adorn the wreath. Propped at the base of the cross, a grapevine wreath bears a bow of red ribbon and faded greenery. A century plant has been incorporated into the memorial by means of a ring of stones, which encircle it and the cross.

Ian Hancock, a university professor who initially described Carrizales's memorial to me, passes it twice every weekday on his way to and from work. He did not know what might have prompted it, however, nor was I able to uncover any relevant information or even a death notice for the deceased in the local newspaper. As indicated on the cross, Carrizales died in 1995. The memorial has been in place since at least early 1996 (Hancock 1997).

Crossroads

As one might expect, many roadside crosses are located at intersections, the sites of many accidents ranging from minor fenderbenders to fatal collisions. Approximately two city blocks to the west-northwest of Sara Jayne Solter's well-known MADD me-

Fig. 3.12 Cross constructed from electrical pole, ceramic insulators, electrical and barbed wire for Armando Carrizales

morial are two crosses at the intersection of William Cannon Boulevard and Manchaca Road. They sit in the drainage ditch of a large
parking lot, adjacent to an arts and crafts megastore and a fast-
food restaurant. That closest to the westbound lanes of Manchaca
Road is constructed of wood painted white with beveled ends,
and is covered almost entirely with multi-colored silk roses in the
manner of the "flowering tree" used in rituals celebrating the
Holy Cross in Mexico and the southwestern United States (Cantú
1991, 118-9, 125; see also McDannell 1995, 121). Two bunches
of artificial daffodils sit at the base. No writing is visible on the
one and one-half by two feet structure.

A yard and a half behind it sits a slightly taller, hollow metal
cross, also painted white. The silver plaque at the crosspiece reads:

> In Loving Memory
> of
> DAREL BRAD GONZALEZ
> October 30, 1977 - June 3, 1995
> We Love You
> Dad, Anna, Brandon & Pee Wee

A ceramic vase at its base holds two bunches of pink and blue silk
roses; another of red daisy-like flowers sits on the ground. Both
crosses were erected by the family following the accident in which
Darel, crossing William Cannon on his bicycle, was hit and then
run over by a truck. Austinite Don Day, who witnessed the accident, confirmed that both crosses were erected in memory of
Darel by the Gonzalez family.

Travelling east on William Cannon and crossing IH-35, motorists pass a white cross and floral display on the southwest corner of the intersection of William Cannon and Rockridge Drive
(Fig. 3.13). Adorned with three red poinsettias and a red bow, a
small, white wooden trellis, and a cross of similar construction
form the southern border of the memorial assemblage. The silk

floral array includes large bouquets of white and red poinsettias, as well as yellow, white, and orange chrysanthemums. Situated next to a fading red fire hydrant at a forty-five degree angle to the roadway, the two-and-a-half-foot cross bears a wreath of multicolored mums at the crossbar. Obscured from the view of passing drivers by the colorful poinsettias are car parts lying in a plastic plant tray at the cross's base.

Although the cross is not marked in any way, judging from the condition of the wooden structures and flowers, it may memorialize a death reported by the *Austin American-Statesman* in September of 1997. Del Valle resident Joe Flores, 28, was driving a motorcycle east on William Cannon when he collided with a truck turning onto Rockridge.

Fig. 3.13 A white cross and trellis are fronted by several floral displays on East William Cannon Boulevard

In May of 1997, I photographed four crosses a mile and a half to the northeast of Darel's memorials, in a median on Stassney Lane directly across the street from David Crockett High School. Seven months later only one remained, minus the myriad items that had encircled it—a small (not quite a foot and a half) white cross in memory of Jacorey Williams, an eight-year-old who was hit by a car on his way home from school (Osborn 1996). A picture of Jacorey was taped to the east face, above football cards and notes covered with plastic wrap, and a glow-in-the-dark rosary, all attached with tape (Fig. 3.14). Surrounding the cross was a large collection of stuffed animals, including teddy bears, rabbits, and dogs, as well as a white ceramic angel, an empty green pop bottle, a football on which is written "To: Jacorey, From: Zack," three bunches of silk flowers including white poinsettias, and an unidentifiable plant set in soil in a yellow plastic cup. A miniature koala bear is perched on a thin wooden stick on the east side of the cross.

Gone by the following January were three wooden crosses, unmarked and unpainted, erected about two yards to the east of Jacorey Williams's memorial on Stassney Lane. Not quite eighteen inches high, they faced away from each other to the west, east and south. The cross facing Jacorey's memorial was adorned with a silk flower and greenery, and two gift bows. The one opposite it, facing east, was decorated with flowers and greenery as well. An arrangement of white poinsettias was placed in front of the third cross. The remnants of four potted plants sat amidst an assortment of stuffed bears, rabbits, dogs, and ducks. An ornate, pastel blue metal Celtic cross, rusted from exposure to a rainy Austin spring, lay across a grey bear, resting beside a small, yellow and black rubber ball.

On June 28, 1996, sixteen-year-old Paul Anthony Garcia was struck by two cars after exiting a city bus at the intersection of North Lamar Boulevard and Morrow Avenue. He was on his way to a baseball game at a nearby field. His mother, interviewed by

Fig. 3.14 Stuffed animals surround Jacorey Williams's cross

Austin American-Statesman reporter Nichole Monroe, stated that a cross would be placed at the site. I found the two-foot wrought-iron cross, tipped with silver *fleurs-de-lys*, at the northeast corner of the intersection (Fig. 3.15). The plaque crosspiece bears the deceased's name and dates of birth and death in white lettering, as well as a small black-and-white portrait. Secured in the ground slightly behind the cross is a large two-dimensional baseball on which is painted Garcia's name, baseball number, and the letters "RIP." Red silk roses are stuck in the ground on both sides of the cross, the larger bunch secured by three large rocks.

Further south, near the intersection of Beanna and 26th Streets on the north end of the University of Texas campus is a white,

Fig. 3.15 This wrought-iron cross and larger-than-life baseball
commemorate the death of Paul Anthony Garcia

wooden cross, measuring one-and-one-half by two feet. Facing
the east and westbound lanes of 26th Street, it is anchored in the
median with concrete. Silver plates with black lettering run almost the entire length of each side of the horizontal piece, and
read:

STEPHANIE MALMQUIST
1-11-74—11-24-93

Malmquist, then a sophomore at the university, died as a result of
injuries sustained when her pickup collided with another vehicle
on 26th Street (Granados 1993). I first photographed the cross
in May 1997, at which time a large basket of woven straw bearing
an arrangement of yellow and red silk elephant ears was held in

place on the west side by cement blocks. When I visited the site again in January 1998, the potted plant was gone and a bouquet of fresh flowers lay at the foot of the cross, protected from the elements by a plastic wrapping printed with the words *"Feliz Cumpleaños"* [Happy Birthday]. A prayer candle in yellow glass cast a dim light about the memorial that evening.

Louisana Hernandez Torres and Eloisa Trevino, two Austin women in their seventies, were killed on January 5, 1996 when their car collided with an eighteen-wheel truck at East Martin Luther King Boulevard and Comal Street (about three-fourths of a mile from Malmquist's cross). The vehicles came to rest on the grounds of Oakwood Cemetery (Kelly 1996). It is here that two plain wooden crosses, each decorated with one white and one pink carnation, were driven into the ground in memory of the two women. Although the writing on the easternmost cross has faded so as to be illegible except for the faint abbreviation "SRA." (señora) on the transverse, the other simply states in black ink lettering:

DIED

1/5/96

SRA. TORRES

A rock supports the base. The crosses are two feet away from the cemetery fence, and about the same distance from the roadway, facing Martin Luther King Boulevard at a very slight angle toward the eastbound lanes.

A mile and a quarter to the east of the assemblage for Torres and Trevino, slightly west of the intersection of Martin Luther King and Airport Boulevards, is a covered bus stop. Behind the north-facing shelter, stuck in the ground just beyond the cement is a wrought-iron, Greek cross just over two feet high. The rust forming on the cross is almost covered by the bright red wreath and floral display. Incorporating red ribbons, carnations, and roses, as well as white roses, baby's breath, and miscellaneous greenery, the wreath hangs slightly beneath a more weathered bunch of white silk roses. There are no identifying markings on the memorial.

On the southeast corner of the heavily traversed intersection, another wrought-iron cross sits in a cleared patch of ground some yards away from two fast-food restaurants. A gold bracelet graces the midsection. Blue, white, yellow, and red silk flowers extend from the base, which also includes a funeral spray of silk flowers spelling out the word "DAD," and a blue and white plastic open Bible.

I did not uncover any background information about either of the two memorials at the intersection, or discern from informants that it is considered a dangerous area. However, with sixteen lanes of traffic facing each other here it is not difficult to imagine what might have happened. Passing through the intersection several times during the course of my fieldwork, I often observed drivers peering intently at one or the other of the crosses when stopped at the intersection.

Other memorials mark areas well-known for numerous accidents. Tara Biggs had almost completed her first year of high school when she was killed in an automobile accident on the way home from school. A cross now stands as a memorial to Tara on the northeast corner of the intersection of County Road 620 and Debba Drive, where the collision occurred. Approximately three feet high, the wooden cross with beveled exposed ends and planter base was built by family friend Rockey Piazza (Thatcher 1995).

Several days after Tara's death, Piazza took the cross to the scene of the accident, where a number of Tara's friends and teachers from Lake Travis High School had gathered. One by one, they took turns applying white paint until the entire structure was covered (Biggs 1998). The cross faces westbound traffic on 620. Most noticeable from the road is the profusion of silk flowers that fills the planter and spills out over the sides—yellow, red, and purple tulips, pink dahlias, yellow daffodils, white irises, purple, yellow, and pink pansies, and sunflowers. Almost obscured by the colorful display are a small, white ceramic angel, molded plastic "Lion King" figurines, and a unicorn figurine encased in a snow globe.[4]

A motorist may be able to see the black plaque with white lettering at the center of each side of the top bar, but probably can't read the words:

TARA

NICOLE BIGGS

7/24/80 - 5/2/95

YOU ARE BEAUTIFUL IN EVERY WAY

WE LOVE AND MISS YOU

Above the plaque on the east side of the vertical piece is a sprig of sunflowers, and a note encased in clear plastic gives the following equation:

cara

+

tara

b.f.4.e.

[best friends forever]

Below the plaque, another note from Cara, similarly protected from the elements, is now virtually unreadable save for the final line and signature (Fig. 3.16). Photographs of Tara are thumbtacked to the top of the vertical: on the east side, Tara in dance team uniform; on the west side, above a sprig of silk buttercups, a more formal photo portrait.

Winding Roads and High Speed

Several yards west of Heather Werchan's memorial on the same median stands an older structure erected in memory of thirty-

Fig. 3.16 Tara Biggs's memorial facing oncoming traffic on Farm to Market Road 620 near Lake Travis

two-year-old Frank Beltran. The *Austin American-Statesman* reported that Beltran lost control of his vehicle while fleeing the scene of an accident. Encircled by large stones, the white, wooden cross bears a bronze plate at the transverse which states in black lettering:

In Loving Memories
Frank Beltran
8-31-64 - 5-5-96
R.I.P.

A black-and-white image of Jesus, encased in plastic, is affixed to the vertical piece above the plate with two white thumbtacks. Tacks also hold a similarly protected color photograph of Beltran on the lower part of the vertical, just above a spray of artificial sunflowers in a green plastic vase. Small stones surround the cross and flowers within the larger stone circle.

Three Hyde Park Baptist High School students were killed on May 2, 1991. As the teenagers headed back to school from a lunch break, driver Tammy Franklin lost control of the car on a curve of southbound Guadalupe and hit a tree head-on. The final resting place of the vehicle was marked by a white cross and a spray of flowers adorning the scarred tree. The three unpainted wooden crosses originally erected by classmates of the crash victims were removed twice, an action attributed to "non-believers" by local police (Franklin 1998). Finally, Susan Crane's then-husband constructed an aluminum cross and set it in concrete (Crane 1998).

When I photographed the site in May, 1997, the engraved silver plaque was partially hidden from view by a bouquet including silk daffodils, white carnations, and buttercups (Fig. 3.17). The plaque bears the following inscription:

Fig. 3.17 Cross on Guadalupe commemorating the 1991 deaths of
Nathan Crane, Tammy Franklin and Jeffrey Suggs

In Loving Memory

Tammy Franklin   September 19, 1974—May 2, 1991
Jeffrey Michael Suggs   August 27, 1974—May 2, 1991
Nathan Eugene Richard Crane November 14, 1974—May 3, 1991

The cross is further surrounded with greenery including artificial pine boughs, probably left during the previous Christmas season. Margie, Tammy's mother, and Susan, Nathan's mother, usually place flowers at the site at Easter, Christmas, the anniversary of the accident, and on the teenagers' birthdays. Susan occasionally finds other items at the site that she attributes to visits from Tammy, Jeffrey, and Nathan's high school friends. The spray of pink and white silk lilies secured to the tree with a length of matching lace

Fig. 3.18 A memorial for three teenagers includes the tree that was struck in the accident

was left by Margie (Fig. 3.18). It is her custom to decorate the tree, as it was the impact with the tree that killed Tammy.

Thomas Vannatta is an English teacher at the aforementioned Crockett High School in south Austin, across the street from Jacorey Williams's memorial. Vannatta's traffic safety concerns, which have resulted in political activism (see chapter five), were galvanized by a fatal accident he witnessed in August of 1989 on Camp Ben McCulloch Road in northeastern Hays County. This section of FM 1826 was described to me by one informant as "a really curvy road where people drive way too fast and have lots of accidents." Tami Speir, a fifteen-year-old driver, lost control of her vehicle as she approached a curve while travelling east. The memorial constructed by family and friends for Tami, then a cheerleader at Dripping Springs High School, included a white wooden cross, constructed of two-by-fours, and standing about a foot and a half high (Fig. 3.19).

The maroon plates nailed to each piece stated in beige lettering:

TAMI L. SPIER
88-89
D.S.H.S.
Cheerleader

O-TAMI

When I got to hug you that night
I heard your body tell mine, "I know daddy
but really I'm OK." That moment
and your little sister
is what keeps me going today.

♥ U-DADDY

Fig. 3.19 Memorial cross and stylized tiger paw print for Dripping
Springs High School cheerleader Tami Speir

A plastic bead necklace hung over the plates on the horizontal
piece. The cross was fronted by a large cement paw print—the
Dripping Springs High School mascot is the tiger—painted in
school colors, maroon outlined in gold. Silk greenery and flowers
in purple and pink stood in back of, and beside the cross.

Southwest Parkway, another infamous highway, provides a
shortcut from one of Austin's major north-south roadways, the
Mopac Expressway (also called "Loop 1"), to the highways southwest of the city. It is known to area residents as a particularly
dangerous zone due to frequent drag racing, including one that
ended in the death of Robert Pickwell, age twenty-three. In an
effort to avoid colliding with a vehicle he had come upon unexpectedly, Pickwell swerved, thus losing control of his car (Canales

1997). His brother, Mike, and a family friend, Frank Mendez, erected the white, wooden cross in a parkway median near the accident site. Mike built the cross in the family's garage.

The memorial is identifiable by the black plastic lettering on both sides. Each side of the horizontal reads "In memory of Rob Pickwell," although the letters on the eastern side are almost entirely obscured by a faded Christmas wreath hung over the crosspiece and assembled from artificial pine boughs, pine cones, and poinsettias. A thin piece of string around the vertical is fastened to an empty wicker basket below a length of wide, striped ribbon. The letters and numbers arranged diagonally down the top half of the eastern side spell out "May 1970," the month and year of Pickwell's birth, while the bottom half of the western-facing vertical bears the month and year of his death, "September 1993." Two bouquets of weatherworn poinsettias sit to the side of the cross, next to the remains of a potted plant still wearing its decorative, though faded wrapping. A plastic bunny and sunflower figurine lie among the dry, brown stems. On the other side of the cross, moulded black plastic pieces, perhaps the top and bottom of an air filter enclosure for a carburetor, rest in the tall grass.

Yet another of the area's notoriously dangerous east-west thoroughfares is the previously noted county road FM 620, west-northwest of Austin. Just prior to a long arcing of the road to the north, a squat, white cross faces the northbound lanes. Unique among wooden crosses in the area in its structural embellishment, this two-and-a-half foot memorial was erected for Chris Ann Stackable, age twenty-four. Stackable was driving at high speed when she lost control of her vehicle on a curve and collided with oncoming traffic (Wright 1995). Her passenger, twenty-four-year-old Wendell Wayne Sauls, was also killed.

The cross's vertical piece is topped with a conical motif (as on a white picket fence), and its horizontal ends by subtle cut-outs. The gold-tone plaque at the crosspiece, inset into a built-in frame, includes Stackable's name, dates of birth and death, August 17, 1970 and February 2, 1995, as well as the epitaph "ALIVE IN THE LORD—FOREVER IN OUR HEARTS." A bouquet of pink, white, and purple silk flowers is attached to the bottom half of the vertical by a length of white ribbon.

FM 620 intersects FM 2222 in the hills west of Austin. Closer in to the city, on a sharp curve between Mount Bonnell Road and Loop 360, a cross stands in memory of Robin Conrad Gullacher (Fig. 3.20). Almost four feet tall, with a two-foot cross bar, the white wooden cross bears black etched lettering over much of its face, including Gullacher's name, dates of birth ("12-31-69") and death ("9-26-97"), and a series of three-digit numbers (e.g., 587, 586, 569, 501, etc.). The significance of these numbers is unknown. Five medium-sized stones encircle the base. Gullacher, driving a motorcycle, was killed when he lost control on the curve and hit two oncoming cars.

Another cross described to me by a university student flanks the northbound access road of Interstate Highway 35. She first saw the white cross in the fall of 1997, in the median between the on-ramp and the freeway itself. Gone after only a few days, the cross appeared in its present location about one month later. It commemorated the death of Carmen Cortinas Vela, age thirty-two, in a head-on collision on the interstate (Monroe 1997). Set back against the fence line and parallel to the roadway, it was situated in a stand of cedar trees.

The blue plaque at the cross piece was inscribed with white lettering, obscured from full view by a large red ribbon attached to the vertical, and a garland of artificial poinsettias adorning the length of the transverse. Visible were the words:

Carmen Cortinas Vela
Mother, Daughter, Sister
May 7, 1997

Fig. 3.20 Gullacher cross on FM 2222

Fig. 3.21 Wrought-iron cross at intersection of Westgate and William Cannon Boulevards. (Photo courtesy of Christie Everett)

Several sprays of silk poinsettias were stuck in the ground in front of the cross, as were sprigs of holly. Behind it was a tall bouquet of silk marigolds and leaves in autumn colors—gold, orange, red, and brown.

In a median of west William Cannon, about three miles west of IH-35, stands a white, wrought-iron cross, visible to all four lanes of traffic at a ninety-degree angle (Fig. 3.21). I was unable to connect this cross to a particular accident with any certainty. It may be related to a one-car wreck in 1992, in which two teenagers were killed (Lindell 1992).

Murder Memorial

Not much further east, and unique to the area, is the memorial to murder victim Shawn Albert Deolloz, a white, wooden cross near the intersection of William Cannon and Emerald Forest Drive. Facing the three westbound lanes of William Cannon, it is set in a cement base in the median with a miniature teddy bear tied around the crosspiece with multi-colored ribbon. The cross's black plaque states in white, italicized lettering:

Shawn Albert Deolloz

We brought in a Diamond
April 13, 1975
God took an Angel
August 4, 1996

Though you can't see or touch me—I'll be near,
And if you listen with your heart, you'll hear
All my love around you soft and clear

Mom, Michael, Karrizza, Monica, Family & Friends

Set in a plastic green vase and scattered about the base are white silk carnations. The clear glass vase next to the cross is empty.

The location of the cross is approximately equidistant from Deolloz's former home and the scene of the crime, as reported in the *Austin American-Statesman* on June 8, 1996. William Cannon is the largest, most heavily traversed street between the two locations, perhaps indicative of the family's desire to memorialize Deolloz in as public a manner as possible. While not connected to a traffic fatality, the cross is akin to the drunk driving protests that the MADD crosses represent in its very public and material commemoration of a crime victim.

Patterns of Memory

Deolloz's memorial is part of one of the most remarkable patterns that emerged during the research period. On William Cannon Boulevard alone I documented seven crosses. The street, which runs for about fourteen miles across the city (southeast to west-northwest) does not have a reputation as particularly dangerous. Most markers have been erected since major improvements, including the addition of lanes and bridges, were made to the thoroughfare in the 1980s and early '90s. The distribution of crosses in the area, however, appears to support the general folklore of such markers as indicative of treacherous areas (Foote 1997, 171-2; Henzel 1991, 97-8; Hurt 1997).

Mexican-American Catholics do continue the tradition generally attributed to their Spanish ancestors, which is evidenced by memorials such as Castor's incorporating the crucifix and, at one time, a representation of the Virgin Mary. Hispanic Catholics are by no means the only individuals who erect crosses, however. Nor are they necessarily the most creative or active. Crosses such as those erected for Tara Biggs and Heather Werchan reflect Protestant aesthetics—there are no crucifixes, rosary beads or holy cards attached to or left at these memorials (Milspaw 1986, 119-20, 132)[5]—as well as the influence of the Hispanic culture of the southwestern United States.

People with whom I spoke did not consider the custom an

ethnically or denominationally exclusive one, nor did they voice adherence to any strict aesthetic principles. These views allow creative license in cross construction, decoration and maintenance. However, there are patterns that emerge from examination of the forty-four crosses described here.

The most widely used material for cross construction is wood, wooden crosses comprising eighty percent of the sample. Of these thirty-five, twenty-three, or fifty-two percent, are painted white. The remaining wooden structures that are finished in some way make up seven percent. Sixteen percent of the crosses are fashioned of wrought-iron or metal. Overall, sixty-eight percent of the crosses, whether wood, iron, or metal, are painted white. In correspondence with geographer Cynthia Henzel's observations in northeastern Mexico, most of the crosses are between two and four feet high, with those smaller generally unmarked, unpainted wooden constructions (1991, 101). Except for a few whose vertical and horizontal pieces are of equal length (Greek cross), or whose horizontal is the longest piece, the crosses are usually Latin in form (1991, 100). Rings or similar borders fashioned of stone, or piles of rocks at the base of a cross were present at thirteen, or almost forty-three percent of the assemblages.[6]

Much less common are those seven assemblages which incorporate automobile parts from the wreckage.[7] In these memorials, the grieving process encompasses not only the death site, but in a sense the actual instrument of death. Further, although MADD markers were the only approved memorial of this kind during the fieldwork period, they comprise only three out of the forty-four. Additionally, not all drunk driving deaths are commemorated with official MADD crosses.

Far more frequent than the use of political statements (i.e., the MADD plaque which states that the deceased was killed by a "drunk driver" and serves as a public plea for more severe DWI penalties) are religious expressions. In addition to the cross and its many signifieds, friends and relatives of the deceased have placed

magico-religious items (rosaries, angels, crosses) or verbal decla-
rations ("Alive in the Lord," etc.) at thirteen sites.

Eighty-seven percent of the crosses are accompanied by remembrances of some kind, from the wildflowers atop Robert
Manly's cross on FM 2222 to the stuffed animals and football
trading cards left for Jacorey Williams. Most frequent, at eighty-
four percent, is the proffering of plants, including flowers, grapevine wreaths, and pine cones, variations of which adorn thirty-seven
crosses. Roses, even during the holiday season, appear to be the
most popular flower, and are part of fifteen assemblages. Most
offered are red roses, found at seven sites, with pink or white ones
at four sites each. Carnations, the second-most utilized flower,
were in evidence at thirty-four percent of the memorials, and were
most often red as well.[8]

A number of my informants spoke about decorating memorials for certain holidays, especially in cases in which grave site or-
namentation is restricted. Many of the assemblages, especially those
photographed in December and January, bore evidence of holiday visits in their adornment. In addition to decorative elements
associated with the Christmas season, some memorials incorporate items linked with Easter. Twenty percent of the assemblages,
for example, included one or more bouquets of red or white poinsettias, often accompanied by ornaments, pine cones, wreaths,
holly, or mistletoe. Two memorials were graced with Easter-
themed wreaths, and the fence behind the two crosses erected in
memory of David Crowley (Fig. 3.9) is decorated by, among other
things, plastic Easter eggs. I did not observe any Halloween-ori-
ented objects, such as pumpkin or black cat figurines, nor any
items generally used in area Day of the Dead celebrations (candy
skulls, skeletons, etc.).

At least one memorial site for an accident victim reflects a decision not to commemorate a death that occurred simultaneously.
The accident that killed Chris Ann Stackable also claimed the life
of Wendell Wayne Sauls, for whom there is no cross. As Barrera

notes, "sometimes the memory of how the person died may simply be too painful" (1991, 281). In other cases, family members have participated, in greater and lesser degrees, in memorials erected by others.

Neither do the crosses commemorate only the deaths of crime victims. As noted, in some cases the deceased were judged by city or state officials to be at fault in the accident, although family members may maintain otherwise. Absolute guilt or innocence is not always reflected in the construction or maintenance of the assemblages, however, as will be discussed in the next chapter, such questions or judgments often render the memorials active sites of negotiation. Family and friends often use crosses as a locus for conflicting emotions connected to a fatal incident. At each memorial, different understandings of people and events are constructed and consumed through an ephemeral confluence of item and image.

Items placed at many of the crosses reflect an ongoing dialogue with the deceased (notes, inscriptions on bridge railings), and the continuation of missed celebrations (toys, homecoming mums, graduation tassels). The memorials become representative not only of the mystery of death, but of the deceased themselves, encompassing aspects of both lived experience and abstract thought. Anthropologist Robert Plant Armstrong has written that, "such works [of art] exist in a state of tension between these two poles; being subject and object. It is perhaps in the energy of such interplay that a fundamental "power"—or energy—of the work of affecting presence is to be found" (1981, 5-6). Documenting the "affecting presence" of the assemblages extends beyond the cataloguing of their various parts. Centuries of tradition and innovation in cultural expression are embodied in the signs and symbols used to reclaim sites of tragedy.

CHAPTER FOUR

~~~

Bereavement
Made Manifest

The communicative power that roadside crosses accrue as a result of the tension between private and public, and the recognition of "ordinary" lives and memories, results from contemporary responses to death in North American society. Many scholars and health care practitioners, such as Geoffrey Gorer (1965), Jack Kamerman (1988), Kathy Charmaz (1980), and Phyllis Silverman (1981) have studied such responses in North America and Britain. All note the increasing isolation of bereaved individuals and contributing societal conditions, such as the development, Kamerman writes, of "mechanisms . . . in American society to keep death out of sight and out of minds," (1988, 2). Similarly, Charmaz refers to the "social construction of the denial of death" (1980, 88-96). Indeed, the contemporary experience of loss, even when documented almost four decades ago by Jessica Mitford in her oft-cited *The American Way of Death* (1963), frequently involves the medical establishment and the death care industry in processes that minimize contact between the deceased and her or his survivors.

Writing about the Vietnam Veterans Memorial, Hass outlines the way in which many contemporary Americans experience the death of a relative or friend: "The standard funeral . . . begins with death in a hospital and transportation of the body to a funeral home. There the body is embalmed, dressed, and made up; this process is usually followed by a viewing of the body and a funeral service in the church of the deceased or at the funeral home. The service is most often followed by a smaller burial service at the cemetery" (1998, 76). In nineteenth century America, however, death often took place in the home, as did preparation for burial and visitation by the community. Nearby cemeteries further strengthened the immediacy of death in the sphere of everyday activity (Laderman 1996, 23-37). In the current context of bereavement, the home symbolizes seclusion and detachment from the everyday activity of the public sphere (Rosenblatt, Walsh and Jackson 1976, 46). Roadside crosses and memorial assemblages, by contrast, occupy a space in the *public* landscape, and imagination, in between the home and the often geographically removed modern cemetery. As revealed by my informants' statements, many aspects of unofficial memorial maintenance are further indicative of their interstitial nature, as their continued existence exhibits a combination of tacit civic support and active community involvement.

The Art of Domestic Experience

Viewed as an extension of domestic activity, corollaries to the roadside cross tradition in Texas are observable in the complex of custom and practice that constitute Day of the Dead celebrations throughout Latin America and the United States.[1] Folk art historians Elizabeth Carmichael and Chloë Sayer have studied traditional observances across Mexico. They found that women generally cook the majority of the food items placed on altars and left at the cemeteries. In those families who own bread ovens, the men of the household do the baking after the women have mixed the dough (1991, 18, 78). Freddy Méndez, a resident of La Congregación del Tajín in the state of Veracruz, for example, describes the way in which his mother prepares chocolate ornaments to adorn the house and especially the altar, as taught by her mother and grandmother. Prior to the festival, women across Veracruz produce cooking utensils and incense burners in fired clay for use during the holiday.

I am particularly interested here in the pattern that emerges in the data collected by Carmichael and Sayer, which includes interviews with a number of artists and craftspeople across Mexico variously involved with the yearly observance, as well as an examination of historic travellers' accounts. In general, women are involved in the preparation of items for use inside the home, or at the cemetery. Men, however, are generally engaged in a different range of activities: reciting prayers for the dead (professional "prayer-makers," or *rezanderos*); going from house to house and singing *alabanzas* in groups of four; or performing as *Xantolo* dancers, sometimes dressed as women, in village streets (1991, plate 23A, 81-82).

The public/private, male/female dichotomy is echoed in the St. Joseph's Day activities of Italian-American women described by folklorists Kay Turner and Suzanne Seriff in their 1987 article "'Giving an Altar': The Ideology of Reproduction in a St. Joseph's Day Feast." The altars, cooperatively designed and constructed by women in a small Texas town, are assemblages which connect "sacred and secular realms by providing a locus of communication, a place for the performance of belief in the home" (448). Their manifest meaning is a tangible, edible thanks offered to Saint Joseph in return for succor in a time of family crisis such as illness, debt, or separation. The altar is laden with an abundance of special foods such as *cosi figli*, *cucchidagli* and *canoli*. The formal presentation of the altar occurs after a ritual reenactment of the biblical account of Joseph and Mary's arrival in Bethlehem, in which the Holy Family is played by community members chosen by the woman giving the altar. The reenactment ends with the ritual feasting of the actors and the community, at which time men serve the food prepared by the women.

While the Saint Joseph's Day preparations and presentations are not connected with death custom, the similarities between women's (and men's) creative labor for this and the customs previously described are notable as reflections of an ideology of reproduction. As conceived by Mary O'Brien, the "maternally derived ideology of reproduction foregrounds social practices based on affiliation, concern for others, sharing, caring, gifting, and religious beliefs" (Turner and Seriff 1987, 447; see also Turner 1999). Such practices certainly encompass the work and artistry evident in Day of the Dead home and cemetery decoration, the St. Joseph's Day traditions of Italian-American women and the memorialization of accident victims with roadside crosses as detailed here. Indeed, as Turner and Seriff assert, it is just such practices that ground the feminist ontology developed by Carolyn Whitbeck. Denouncing the necessity of the self-other opposition that pervades western, and largely patriarchal, scholarship, this ontology is defined as "the mutual realization of people" (Turner and Seriff 1997, 458). Whitbeck's examples include "nursing and caring for the sick, disabled and elderly, . . . counseling and various forms of spiritual practice" (1984, 75). While St. Joseph's Day traditions stem from the desire to acknowledge the saint's intervention in the past, the aforementioned death customs concern the immediate spiritual needs of grieving individuals and communities.

Personalized spiritual practice, when based and performed in the home, may also be viewed as vernacular religion (Primiano 1995, 44), or the "domestication of religion" (Sered 1988, 516). Both imply an active manipulation of religious tenets or iconography for highly personal use, and thus are closely related to materials or built environments studied by folklorists and others as examples of "vernacular architecture." Indeed, as folklorist Leonard Primiano states, "[T]he beliefs of individuals themselves radiate and influence the surrounding environments. The verbal, behavioral, and material expressions of religious belief mean a variety of instruments and occasions of expressive culture which can be categorized under the rubric of visual or performed arts, public and private cultural performances, and individual acts. These would include but not necessarily be exhausted by the following: speech, music and song, dance, mime, ritual and drama, bodily communication, the manifold uses of writing, foodways, costume, culturally encoded architecture, and *the permanent and ephemeral objects within domestic and public environments*" [emphasis added] (44-45). Moreover, Primiano recognizes the presence of the vernacular not only in the domestic, which often assumes a degree of privacy, but in the public sphere as well.

Correspondingly, it is the ephemeral aspects and objects of built environments that historian Angela Kwolek-Folland singles out for attention in gendered analyses of vernacular architecture. She writes that "many contributions to vernacular architecture are ephemeral, a fact particularly true in the case of women. In our historical experience of gender, the trappings and interior decorations of buildings, some of which are seasonal, are important to the meaning and experience of vernacular space" (1995, 6). Certainly the extension of the scope must also include, in the case of material culture studies, the ephemeral in more public settings, specifically the ways in which women and men (re)create and (re)present various events and ideas in ritual altars, yard art, shrines, and memorials.[2]

Analytical Intersections

Excessive speed may have been a factor in the accident that killed Shilah Lamay's daughter, Heather, and Bowie High School classmate Lisa Wendenburg in 1996. Lisa was driving the car when she apparently lost control of the vehicle. It crossed the center line of Manchaca Road, and hit another car. Heather, who was in the passenger seat, died at the scene. Lisa died the following day (Hoppe and Gonzalez 1996). Shilah said, "they were killed Saturday afternoon, Saturday night there was a cross put up, made by the kids that night." The two crosses, one for Heather and one for Lisa, no longer stand at the accident site, due to a road-widening project. At the request of the Texas Department of Transportation, Shilah and her husband, John, first moved the assemblage back a few yards, to the fence line of the nearest property owner. Later they removed the crosses as well, leaving a granite piece bearing an etching of the two women, and a wreath. Shortly before I interviewed Shilah in May 1997, they removed the granite and wreath in preparation for a move to another state.

Shilah identified a classmate and friend of the two young women as the driving force behind the memorial. She said, "There were two temporary crosses that the kids wrote all over. And basically what they wrote on those crosses was all goodbye notes, and we have one of those crosses. I mean we took those down simply because they were not going to last. Her best friend is the one . . . they made a cement cross and it had the girls' names on it, and that's, you know, they put that up and put a heart around it. They did all that. We didn't have a thing to do with it. What we did do, though, at the site, was we had two, a granite picture made with just the girls' picture on it." Shilah's reference to the "heart around it," concerns the heart-shaped border, fashioned out of nearby rocks, laid around the white, cement cross. The east-facing memorial, constructed at the spot where Lisa's car came to rest, quickly became a gathering place for Lisa and Heather's friends.

Local teacher Linda Boyd spoke of seeing groups of teenagers at the memorial for several weeks after the accident, as she drove home from work in the afternoon. Area teenagers reported seeing offerings such as beer bottles and coins at the site. When I asked Shilah about items left there, she said, "Yeah, there were coins. They would leave cigarettes. . . . . Of course, they've always left flowers. I would go every once in a while and see a single rose. We had "The Rose," that song, sung [for Heather], and my husband had sent her a dozen red roses the day before at school, and so the rose, anything with rose has always [been] pretty special . . . I notice that if it's kids who are leaving something for Heather, they'll usually leave a rose, you know." Items were left at the site up until the time that the cross was removed. In addition, the teens planted a small flower bed, also bordered by rocks.

Shilah emphasized the fact that the memorial was the kids' enterprise in statements such as: "Essentially . . . that was unrelated to us. I mean, we did not have anything to do with it." However, her comments also revealed that she and her husband spent a great deal of time visiting the site in an effort to show support for the victims' friends. In keeping with Mary O'Brien's ideology of reproduction (1981), Shilah and John showed concern for the teenagers in a time of crisis for all involved. John was especially worried about the reaction of Lisa and Heather's friends. Shilah explained, "My husband was, more so than me, he was very concerned about making sure that some of these kids, they had lost two friends earlier in the year, and so he was more concerned, 'I don't want these kids, somebody to, you know, to try to commit suicide.' So we went there, and spent two nights with the kids. We went on Monday night right after she was killed and I believe it was Tuesday night we stopped by." Although the cross, as a symbol, was not important to the Lamays, they considered it essential to be present at the memorial for the emotional well-being of the young people gathering there.

Bowie students lost another classmate in May of 1997, in the one-car wreck that claimed the life of Heather Werchan. Like the memorial for Lamay and Wendenburg, the large cross on Slaughter Lane bearing Heather's name was constructed and installed by classmates rather than by family members. Her father, James, said, "As far as Heather's, it never, we had never thought about it . . . her friends that she ran around with, she dated two boys in that group. And they were good friends. They were the ones that actually, together they put the cross up. They decided to put the cross up and it was, I guess it was probably about a week after the accident or after the funeral that they put it up. They decided to put it up."

The Werchans were not upset by the young men's decision to memorialize Heather publicly. Moreover, he and his wife, Ruby, assumed care of certain aspects of the site. In addition to changing the floral displays seasonally, James explained that, "It's a grass median. There's a wide median there. And I mow the grass, you know, on the other side of the tree and a pretty good ways back away from the cross toward Bowie [High School]. So I keep it looking nice and maintain it." Ordinarily, city crews mow such medians. As James reveals here, not only have Heather's family and friends utilized city property for her memorial, they have also taken over its maintenance.

The Werchan family now finds the cross a consoling presence. As lifelong Lutherans, they are comfortable with the cross's symbolism. In contrast, Shilah thinks that the cross, as a Christian symbol, was not particularly meaningful to Heather and Lisa's friends. When I asked if those who had constructed and visited it were practicing Christians, Shilah laughed and said, "Very definitely not. Very definitely not her friends, you know. No. . . . I don't think the cross itself from a Christian standpoint has any significance to these kids. I think they see it more as a memorial, yeah. And see, even for us, from our perspective, a cross to me is, it can easily be an idol . . . . to me the spiritual part of this is something inside of us. I don't see it as things from the outside. And so for us that's why, in a sense even though we may be Christians, the cross isn't necessarily a form of any meaning to me at a personal level. But, no, definitely . . . based on a few of the other people I know, it doesn't seem to be related at all to kids who tend to be Christians."

Even in light of their views about the cross and its place in her family's beliefs, she and John wanted to support the young people in the maintenance of the assemblage. Their relationship with Heather and Lisa's friends may be understood as mutually achieved, rather than oppositional, or self-other (Whitbeck 1984). The teens' use of a symbol which holds little meaning for Shilah and John, and perhaps negligible meaning for themselves in Shilah's assessment, did not preclude cooperative participation in the construction of the memorial. Indeed, Shilah and John's informal counsel of the teens, which I interpret as reproductive labor, extended beyond participation in the memorial to their home. As Shilah explained, even after she felt that her family was ready to "move on," grieving youths continued to stop by their house.

Further, Shilah considered the concern for the teenagers' emotional well-being to be more her husband's than her own. She stated that, "Even after [Heather] was killed, I tended to focus in more on my three kids, whereas my husband . . . also kind of included the other kids, you know, her friends." Nonetheless, she went with him to visit the memorial in the days following the accident, and on subsequent occasions such as the first anniversary of Heather's death.

Likewise, the anniversary visit to the accident site was made, at least in part, in response to the needs of someone other than herself. Shilah commented, "Well, this last January was the year anniversary. And I said to John, 'I just really feel like I want something there on that year anniversary.' Because it was blank. So, I had a little wreath made and then, kind of cowboy-like, and it said 'In Loving Memory of Heather and Lisa' and then we put the girls', the little granite piece back up. . . . We had a lot of things going on that day, but we just felt like we wanted to put something so it wasn't just blank on the anniversary. And, it was just a way of us knowing we remembered her, you know. And I think a lot of kids were calling us at that time and asking us, you know, where the stuff was and if it was going to be able to go back in."

Shilah and John, in their participation in the roadside memorial, took roles as caretakers of both womens' memories. Lisa's family was not involved in the construction or maintenance of the site. The granite piece depicting both women was ordered and installed at the site by the Lamays, as was the wreath Shilah had made a year later. Thus, the Lamays labored not only to preserve the memory of both their daughter and her friend, but to support the friends they left behind. Shilah made all concerns her own.

Her attention to the accident site, evident in her desire that it not be "blank" on the anniversary, was echoed in comments made by Heather Werchan's father, James, and Nathan Crane's mother, Susan. In all three accidents, the driver lost control of the vehicle, and in the case of Werchan and Crane, the cars collided with trees. Marking the accident site, therefore, entails the public recognition of responsibility to no small degree. The cross for Heather was made by two friends, one of whom, Christopher Johnston, was driving the car at the time of the accident. Regardless of the cross's origin, Werchan knows that "one way or another we would still go down that road. And it's always nice and comforting to see that there." Elaborating further, he stressed the significance, both positive and negative, of the site, "You know, we'd never want to forget about her. So, you know, just because that's there we wouldn't, if it wasn't there we wouldn't forget about her anyway. But it's just a nice tribute to her. And even though, unfortunately, it had to happen. But it was her time to go home anyway, to see her heavenly father."

James understands Heather's death as ultimately purposeful. Therefore, the responsibility for the accident rests with God, rather than with Johnston. Christopher and his mother also help decorate and maintain the memorial site. James said, "[S]he just replaced the letters. They were, I think they were dark green letters, I think, before. Now they're yellow and she painted flowers on them. And she planted, they planted a little miniature rose shrub next to it also." Caring for the site—constructing its meaning and thus the meaning of the accident—also involves the construction and negotiation of role and responsibility.

Margie believes that because the circumstances of the accident that killed Tammy, Nathan, and Jeff were somewhat mysterious, it was predestined. Noting that there were no other cars involved and no witnesses came forward, she said, "God had a certain amount of days for Tammy. She was in heaven the instant she died." While authorities maintain that Tammy was speeding when she lost control of the vehicle, Margie says she knows "that isn't true." During our conversation, she stressed Tammy's driving skills, the fact that she had taken driving lessons and that she was the best driver of all Margie's children, regardless of what I or others might have read in the newspaper.

As Margie continues to struggle with the circumstances of her daughter's unexpected death, she also grapples with the knowledge that two other youths (Nathan and Jeff) died in the accident. She stated that Nathan's mother, Susan, has continued to be friendly toward the Franklin family since the accident, alluding to the fact that Susan does not openly blame Tammy or her family for Nathan's death. Both Susan and Margie, however, mentioned that Jeff's mother reacted rather more negatively.

In the course of our discussion about the memorial for Tammy, Jeff, and Nathan on Guadalupe Street, Susan Crane said, "I wanted something there that was a connection. I didn't want it to be just a lost place. To me that was not, it is a place of violence, but it was not, to me it was more of a, well like I said the last place where I feel like the spirit was last. It's not, I mean, I don't think Jeff's mother, I think that she was very angry about it. So that I know that would not be a place of endearment for her. You know, and I, to say endearment is a horrible word, because a place of a death is not an endearing place." Regardless of the circumstances of her son's death, Susan wished to mark the spot for herself as the teenagers' friends first had. At the same time, she helped provide a place for the school community to grieve.[3]

The site is approximately two miles from the school that the three teenagers attended, a private, religious institution that attracts students from across the city. Like the Lamays, Susan worried about the emotional impact of the fatalities on the student body at large, saying, "I guess one other thing that that cross does, is it, well I've already mentioned that, but to me, it was traumatic for me. And I knew that it was for those kids at school and a lot of things that I did, not only were for me, but I wanted to do them for the kids at school. Because I wanted them to have a way to deal with it." Susan did not have a partner at the time of Nathan's death; however, dealing with the tragedy was far from a solitary endeavor.

Although Susan and Margie often redecorate their parts of the memorial independently, their labor, or "grief work" applies to the school community at large.[4] Both women believed it important to include the tree that was struck in the assemblage. Susan explained, "You know, since that was the scene of the accident and the tree that's there, if you notice the tree the bark is off. And that was from the accident. In the photo that I have of the wreck that was in the paper . . . you can see the different kind of things there. They had the IVs and things for the children while they were trying to get the jaws of life to get them out. They had that hanging from the tree, and I know a lot of the kids went there or were aware of that. So I think that a lot of them went there to deal with the emotions that they had." While Susan admits that it was a traumatic time for her, she reveals that she was thinking about the accident victims' friends as well—what they had seen or heard, and how they might have been affected. She recognized their need to grieve and attempted to address it through the transformation of the accident site into a memorial.

Similarly, Vicki Biggs believes the memorial constructed at the scene of her daughter Tara's accident to be an important place for the entire community. It plays an integral part in the grieving process, she noted, saying, "I think it's a big part of the process for people. . . . what it does is give people—kids, adults, whatever—a place to go. . . . [Tara's] friends tell me all the time that when they're feeling down or they've got a problem or whatever that they'll go up there and sit at the cross. And then they'll feel better when they leave. So I feel like to them it's, it's a place to go, someplace that they feel like Tara's still there, you know, and I, it's hard to explain."

The cross was cooperatively constructed, and still bears the imprint of many hands—the notes from Cara, the plaque that reads "We love and miss you." Vicki has taken over most of the responsibility for the maintenance of the assemblage now, and said that she and her husband, Ronnie, and her daughter, Crystal, decorate more at the cross than at the cemetery.[5]

Tara's classmates continue to contribute to the site, as well. Vicki told me, "That cross, up there, really means a lot to the kids. The kids go up there a lot. When it's holidays, or it's anniversaries, or, it's just like here at Christmas. I went up there and put poinsettias out, and decorated it, you know, for the holidays, for Christmas and put a candy cane, and this and that. Well, I had several people calling me wanting to do something. One of her best friends went up and put garland, you know, around the cross, and another one came up and brought a little angel."

Additionally, her commitment to the public nature of the assemblage is such that she has not been troubled when something has been taken away. She said, "The only thing that ever happened, and I think—'cause during football season each year, the Cavalette moms do mums for all the Cavalettes.[6] And they're all alike and everything, so we always do one for Tara and hang it on the cross. And then I always bring it back home and then Crystal keeps it as a keepsake and stuff. And when I went up there to get it, it was gone. Somebody had taken it. But nothing else was touched. So I really feel like somebody took it that knew Tara. That it wasn't stealing it, they really wanted it as a keepsake for them. Other than that, no one's ever touched anything up there, which makes me happy as can be."

The act of taking a memento from the cross is in agreement with Vicki's conception of the site, even if an item is removed anonymously. She understands it to be a place where many people go to feel close to Tara, saying "I've driven by and seen cars stopped there and some of the kids up there, or, they tell me all the time, like, one of her friends, Jamie, she says she goes up there and talks to her all the time. She said, you know, anything big going on in her life and she goes up there and asks her to be her guardian angel and to pray for her and make, help her get through it, or whatever. They kind of use that as, everybody . . . that knew Tara, that were close to Tara, which was a lot of people!" Her efforts to maintain the memorial emphasize her acknowledgment of the community's participation in her grieving process, and she in theirs, a mutual realization that honors the needs of bereaved individuals and groups, such as Tara's dance team, the Cavalettes. The Werchans understand Heather's memorial similarly. James has noted that although the site has never been disturbed, nor have items been taken away, he regularly finds other offerings.

The seasonal, or event-centred nature of the decorating that is done at roadside memorials—such as placing a custom-made homecoming mum at a cross during football season—underscores the transitory nature of the assemblages, as does the very real threat of destruction due to roadway construction, safety considerations, or vandalism.[7] Moreover, the ephemeral nature of the memorial sites facilitates participation. As noted by folklorists Turner and Jasper with regard to Day of the Dead grave site decoration customs in Texas, ". . . participants in the tradition know that their offerings inevitably will be consumed by time and nature. Someone who buys an impermanent product will have reason to return . . . ." (1994, 145). The maintenance of an outdoor memorial assemblage, including items such as fresh and artificial flowers, stuffed animals, and notes, necessitates regular attention. Thus the memorials represent the construction and consumption

of memory, while simultaneously acting as a reflection of the at-
tendants' own lives.

Religious beliefs are bound up in the expressions of everyday
life—a white cross, facing east, adorned with plastic beads, or a
note from a friend. While Shilah may question the value of the
cross in her spiritual practice and those of her daughter's friends,
James, Margie, Susan, and Vicki embrace the cross as a symbol of
hope. Tara's grave site at a non-denominational cemetery happened to be in the shadow of a white, fifteen-foot-high cross.
Vicki explained that she and her husband had not previously known
where Tara would be buried, as they had purchased the family
plots some years earlier. When they went to see the site, following
the accident, Vicki asked to see the plot. She said, "And so they
took us out there, and I went, 'What more appropriate?' I mean,
she's buried right there below that big cross. And I was like,
'Wow!'" Although, as Vicki says, her family is not "very, very,
very religious," they hold firm Christian beliefs. Elaborating, she
said, "We do go to church. We don't go to church every Sunday.
We believe, you know, that you don't necessarily have to go to
church to believe and to be a Christian. Yes, you should be
[laughs], but with our lives . . . we make excuses. But we, we're
very religious and we believe that Tara's in heaven and we're going to see her. One of these days." The cross, and the decorating
that accompanies it, has become an integral part of Vicki's expression of spiritual convictions.

The cross constructed for Tammy, Jeffrey, and Nathan is viewed
similarly by Margie Franklin and Susan Crane. Susan wanted the
cross to face east, "because Jesus will come back in the east."
Additionally, in Christian belief the cross signifies death-as-transi-
tion. Susan explained, "I'm Baptist, because of the fact that I
believe in, in when you die you go straight to heaven, somehow
or another the cemetery did not hold anything for me. I mean, I
do flowers at the cemetery also, but . . . to me, the last place that
Nathan was was at that tree. You know, that was, the symbolism is

there and even though I go to the cemetery, I don't, it didn't seem like that was where I was drawn because he's not really at the cemetery. For some reason or another this location is where he was, so I would go there and I wanted to put a cross there because that was where I went the most. And so I guess the symbolism is that that's kind of where I felt his spirit was last." In accordance with her religious beliefs, Susan views the accident site, marked with the cross, as more hopeful and comforting than the cemetery. Like Susan, Margie feels connected to the accident site because it was where her daughter was last alive on this earth. She said, "that's where everything ended and began."

Margie attributes her continuing desire to maintain the site to her gender, saying "I know it has a lot to do with being a woman, [you want to] make sure everything's in order." Susan, especially, has taken great care with the decorating, even going so far as to make arrangements with someone else to change the flowers when she has been unable to do it: "I'm in the process now, once it gets a little enough away from Christmas, I'm going to do the January flowers. Of course, I'm fixing to go into the Valentine's Day flowers. I have been doing seasons. Each of the holidays and things like that. There's been a time or two when I've been out of town and I've put something there and it kind of disappeared right away, or something like that, or I thought someone, I was going to have someone else do it for me and they either didn't get there or whatever . . . if I could not go there, then I had arranged for someone else to take it over there for me, if I was out of town." Every time she changes the flowers at the cross, she tries to change them at the cemetery as well.

Margie, Susan, James, and Shilah all spoke of cleaning or reorganizing the assemblages. Susan said, "You know, the flowers have been—one time, one Christmas several years back, the flowers and things that are there, someone threw them everywhere, the little tree and everything that I'd put. They were, I couldn't find them, I had to start all over and finally I found them. And occasionally, I found them off in the bushes where they used to have trash there. And occasionally the grounds keepers would find things and bring them back and put them over there for me." James and his wife, Ruby, have assumed care of certain aspects of Heather's memorial as well. In addition to changing the floral displays seasonally, James mows the grass in the median, a task he has apparently taken over from city maintenance crews. Shilah and her husband regularly checked the site of Heather and Lisa's cross for refuse. Shilah explained, "We asked the kids, I said, 'Please keep the trash, you know?' Lot of smokers. . . . so we would, my husband and I, one of us would kind of try to like, on a weekly basis, you know, stop by and make sure that things were kept clean." Labor included not only providing decorative elements, but maintaining the overall orderliness of the memorial site, as one might straighten up one's own home or yard.

Folklorist Grey Gundaker, in a study of Halloween and other decorations in an Alabama cemetery, writes that the life and death symbolism of the holiday, together with the traditional images (angels, praying hands, lambs) found in graveyards, helps "construct interlocking worlds and open lines of communication for the living, the dead, and the spirits in between" (1994, 263).[8] Displays more often associated with home and yard adornment, she asserts, allow bereaved individuals to incorporate the dead into the world of the living, and vice versa—a function also performed by roadside memorial assemblages. Changing the flowers, seasonal items and even the figurines or photos left at memorial crosses keeps the memory of loved ones highly accessible and vital.

Grief Work

In a quantitative study of seventy-eight cultures, Paul Rosenblatt, Patricia Walsh, and Douglas Jackson documented emotional responses to death, including crying, anger, self-mutilation, aggression toward others, and fear (e.g., fear of a corpse, fear of ghosts). Their survey, which included groups as far-flung as Thai villagers, Pawnees, Trobrianders and Egyptian Fellahins, did not produce results as disparate as one might expect. In fact, the trio's work serves as confirmation of certain gender stereotypes: women tend to cry more frequently, while men more often express themselves through anger and aggression (1976, 144-46). Also noted are various tie-breaking rituals of "destroying, giving away, or temporarily putting aside personal property of the deceased" (68). What the authors do not address, however, are ways in which grief manifests itself in the *production* (or offering) of material goods.

Items left at civil structures like the Vietnam Veterans Memorial, altars such as those connected with Day of the Dead celebrations, and roadside memorial assemblages materially express profound feelings of loss and remembrance. The remembrances speak not only to the creator(s) of the assemblage, but to family and friends, and often to the wider community.

Thanatologist Phyllis Silverman, in a study of widows, battered women, and young birthmothers who have given their children up for adoption, attributes the severe and often debilitating depression experienced by women in mourning to the inability of western society to acknowledge and support the bereaved. Grieving women, Silverman believes, suffer a double loss, losing the part of their identity based on their relationship with the deceased, and societal support at the same time (1981, 23). The key is to develop a new identity as part of the grieving process (Kamerman 1988, 72). According to psychologist Erich Lindeman, the timely completion of grief work results in "emancipation from the bondage to the deceased, readjustment to the environment in which the deceased is missing, and the formation of new relationships" (qtd. in Kamerman: 66). The work of those who have lost someone unexpectedly, however, is often rendered especially difficult (Charmaz 1980, 142, 289-291). Kamerman links the inability of many bereaved individuals to accomplish meaningful grief work to the paucity of meaningful death-related rituals available in the western context.

His statements reiterate the pleas of Rosenblatt, Walsh, and Jackson for either the ritualization of death customs already practiced to some degree in the United States, or more widespread acceptance of the rituals, whether grounded in formal religious or civil culture or not, that individuals and groups have developed for themselves in order to work through loss in a more timely and successful fashion (1976, 109-11). It may be, though, that the lack of codified mourning rituals in North American society bemoaned by psychologists and sociologists has left individuals cultural space in which to fashion their own.[9] An increasing number of individuals, women and men, in Austin have adapted and reshaped a custom with roots in the European conquest of the Americas into an extension of the reproductive labor they are accustomed to performing in and around the home.

In south Texas, Turner and Jasper have found that Day of the Dead activities center on cemetery cleaning and decoration, which clearly "demarcate the difference between the living and the dead" (1994, 140). The authors stress the social impulse anchoring the annual event in community practice. While the dead are remembered and honored, so too are extant community ties between family and friends reaffirmed. In their self-assigned grief work, the individuals I interviewed have engaged in an analogous process of reifying relationships and personal convictions—acts of regeneration (Turner and Jasper 1994, 149). The construction and maintenance of memorial assemblages has allowed them to incorporate their memories of, and abiding affection for, their loved ones into the everyday life of their families (Zimmerman 1997, 5). Simultaneously, they have sustained the community ties the deceased may have had in life by (re)creating a public site which friends may visit anonymously and quickly, by simply driving past.

As memorials, roadside crosses are symbolically representative of on-going grief work. In contrast to the successful grieving process envisioned by Kamerman, Lindemann, and others, however, they do not always reach a state of closure. This is not to say the assemblages, or those who create them, have been unsuccessful, or failed in any sense. As Silverman writes, "The past is not cut out of the person's life and renounced, but rather the person changes [their] relationship to it. The gap between the past life and the future life is bridged more easily when elements of the past are incorporated into the present, but with an altered emphasis" (1981, 28). Indeed, the memorials depict a more fluid understanding of life, death and the respective role of memory in shaping both spatial and temporal experience. Vicki estimates that she drives past Tara's cross an average of ten times as she goes about her daily routine, saying, "But I go by there so much, now, that, you know, I just—I know this is going to sound silly, but as I go by, I go, 'Hi, sweetie!' And I just keep on driving. So, you know, no, it doesn't bother me, I guess. I guess, in a way, it makes me feel better. Makes me feel closer to her because she's, she's out here." Tara is still an important part of Vicki's life.

CHAPTER FIVE

Cross Connections,
Social Meanings

Folklorists such as William Bascom have emphasized the integrative functions of traditional culture—validation, the maintenance of conformity, education, and entertainment. In addition, many folkloric forms, such as roadside crosses, function as agents of economic integration and social levelling. It is important to note, however, the non-integrative, or subversive consequences of traditional culture as well.[1] It is precisely in such *counter-hegemonic* expression that grieving individuals often find voice. Thus, roadside cross assemblages require a modified functionalist analysis.

The following discussion is primarily based on data obtained from questionnaires I administered to approximately one hundred high school seniors.[2] Additionally, I drew from interviews with individuals connected to and employed by city, county, and state governmental entities, as well as a random sampling of area residents. The analysis also incorporates the words and ideas of individuals introduced in the third and fourth chapters.

Validation and Conformity

The crosses "perform" the function of validation in their public representation of generally accepted, or at least tolerated religious belief. As noted in chapter two, Travis County's largest religious group consists of adherents to Roman Catholicism, at 48.4% of the total population (Ramos 1997, 489). Christian belief and its general acceptance by area residents are manifest in the proliferation of religious symbols such as roadside crosses. The fact that they are infrequently vandalized is further evidence of tacit approval.[3] Interestingly, however, only a small number of questionnaire respondents cited religious belief in their assessments of the crosses.

Some of these include high school student Jenny Stinson, who wrote that the crosses "remind me that I could die in a heartbeat and I have to be in the right standing with the Lord." Another student noted seeing "crosses signifying that the person was or is Christian." One individual defined roadside memorials as "a white cross with usually flowers or a picture of Jesus."

More explicit statements of personal belief came from a student who wrote that she contributes prayers to such sites. Another stated that "when I pass a marker that I know something about, I usually say a quick little prayer of friendship." Debbie Wimberly, a friend of Heather Lamay and Lisa Wendenburg's, wrote "When I pass the site I turn off the radio and remember Lisa and Heather with a prayer" (1997a). Interviewed by phone, she elaborated, saying that she also prays "for everybody to watch after everybody else" (1997b). For Debbie, Jenny, and the other teenagers quoted above, the crosses function similarly to the *descansos* and traveler's shrines described by Barrera, Griffith, Henzel, and West, as special places at which one may offer prayers not only for the deceased, but for the living as well, regardless of denominational affiliation.

American civil religion underlies the broad, tacit acceptance and validation of Christian belief as evidenced by the custom of erecting roadside crosses. While they may not represent the exact beliefs associated with their origins in Mexico and the American southwest (e.g., persons dying suddenly without the benefit of last rites require assistance, in the form of prayers, in order to find peace after death), those expressed by my informants are all basic to various Christian doctrines.

Conformity to the beliefs associated with roadside crosses, as well as adherence to traditional commemorative aesthetics, inform and regularize memorial design (Barrera 1991, 279-80; McDannell 1995, 120-123). As documented here, the most common roadside memorial in the Austin area consists of a wooden cross, painted white, with some form of identifying lettering at the crosspiece. The crosses are often accompanied by bouquets of silk flowers. Not surprisingly, questionnaire respondents and other informants frequently noted the pattern, writing "I see many small white crosses usually with flowers." One student compared markers in Austin with others s/he has seen in Mexico: "Most of the markings I've seen consist of crosses decorated with flowers and religious pictures. I've also seen small chapel-like structures in Mexico which have a gate that open so that you can put gifts inside." Another student described those she saw most often, along with variations, "They are white crosses about two to three feet high. They usually have [plastic] flowers around them or on them, and sometimes even stuffed animals or letters or dedications on them."

Contributing decorative or personally meaningful items to the assemblages is another aspect of the custom. Several questionnaire respondents outlined their own participation, writing that they, or friends of theirs, had given money toward the cost of a cross or plaque, or left bouquets of flowers, candles, stuffed animals, or other toys at various sites. One student stated that she "wrote a little message on the cross" erected for Heather Lamay and Lisa Wendenburg. Debbie Wimberly recalled that friends of Heather's once took a case of beer to the cross, and would sometimes drink half of one and pour the rest on the ground.[4]

Education

Certainly roadside crosses perform an educational role, serving as powerful, indexical signs of tragedy which emphasize the hazards of routine vehicular travel. Their presence on city streets travelled by thousands every day underscores the danger that a society enamored of automobiles tends to disregard in favor of cars as symbols of "freedom and independence" (Steinhart 1983, 346). The intersection that now features a memorial for Tara Biggs was known throughout the community as a dangerous one for years prior to the accident that killed her. When I asked Vicki Biggs if she and Tara's friends think of the cross as a warning, she replied, "It was so funny because after the accident happened, that cross was there, kids and parents would come up and say they would automatically slow down, every time, when they got to that spot. Not only because they wanted to see her cross, but because it was a warning."

Vicki finds comfort in the fact that Tara's cross may remind people to proceed through the intersection more cautiously. Whereas the cross's initial purpose was to memorialize Tara, it became an important, informal road sign. Later in the interview, Vicki said, "You know, when something first happens, everybody is just really, you know, 'I'm never gonna speed, I'm never gonna do this, I'm not gonna do that, I'm gonna pay attention, I'm gonna'—but then, as time goes along, you start getting back into your old habits and going right back into, you know, being reckless and thinking you're invincible. And, it, I think it helps to bring that back to them. Every time they pass there they see that cross and realize 'I'm not invincible, I do need to take care of myself.' And if, there was a lot of positives that came from that, and those are a few of those positives, that as long as they continue to do that, then I mean, there's a meaning behind everything that happens." Viewing the crosses as cautionary and potentially life-saving helps those who have lost a loved one in a fatal collision locate meaning in an otherwise senseless death.

Shilah Lamay considers the element of warning an important part of the custom of erecting roadside crosses, and acknowledges that it was a factor in her response to the cross constructed for her daughter, Heather. She said, "I think sometimes too, some people put them up because they think, 'will it make somebody slow down, will it make somebody think before they go around that corner too fast?' Now in our case, that's a part of it."

Although they did not participate in the construction of the original crosses erected for Heather and her friend Lisa, Shilah and her husband came to value the memorial's educational, as well as its emotional value. Similarly, James Werchan said, "[H]aving it there is really good. You know, because it is a reminder for two things. Of Heather, of course, and the other is for people just to slow down and be more cautious, too, of people that are dying because of traffic accidents." He regards his daughter Heather's cross as both a memorial and a lesson.

Margie Franklin also expressed the hope that the cross for her daughter, Tammy, and her friends on Guadalupe Street will always be a "reminder to people to be careful." Although it was not an integral part of her desire to erect a cross, Susan Crane now considers the cross to be a warning as well as a tribute. She said, "[I]t immortalizes them, so that they, even though you know that they're not in your life anymore, nobody's going to forget them. And, possibly, I think, and of course a lot of the crosses are DWI crosses. But even still sometimes a cross, and people, you know, like these they said, 'Why do you have this 'Ice on the Bridge' sign, when you haven't had ice here? And they said, 'So that you'll be aware of it.' But a lot of times, by having it there, you take it for granted. But, a lot of times, too, a lot of people have told me 'when I see that, I always say a prayer for my children,' or for such and such children, or for the children, you know. It reminds them that, you know, that you have to be safe when you're driving." Susan recognizes that while they may also be read as cautionary, the roadside memorials speak in a markedly different way than official highway signage, inspiring emotional as well as intellectual responses.

Passersby draw their own conclusions regarding the message of a given marker. Questionnaire respondents who did note reactions to the memorials wrote that the crosses reminded them to "slow down," "drive safely," or "to be a careful driver." One discussed "the decline of responsibility when it comes to drivers" and wondered "what happened; if it was anyone's fault; if it could have been avoided." "[Seeing a roadside cross] makes me more alert when driving because obviously someone else wasn't," wrote another student. A similar sentiment was expressed by the statement "I get depressed because it's hard to believe how careless some drivers can be and also how careless people walking or whatever can be." Here, the writer extends responsibility for traffic safety to pedestrians and perhaps bicyclists. Further, to some respondents the crosses suggest the need for civic action, such as the woman who discussed the Jacorey Williams accident with her mother: "She [mother] thought it was sad and thinks the bus ought to stop on the other side of the road since that's where the apartments are."

Student Maegan Wheeler lost a relative to a traffic accident. As a result, she feels "weird" when passing any roadside cross, she says, because, "I mean, I've had someone in my family die in a car wreck. And it's such a big deal to you and your family. But then, like, after it's over and you know . . . everything's cleaned up and all you see is that cross. Anybody else driving along, it's like, 'Oh, there's just a cross.' It's so weird that it can mean so little to one person, and so much to . . . a whole family of the person that died." Although a cross was not erected at the site of the accident in which her relative was killed, Maegan thinks such memorials are a good idea. "I think it is, because it makes you think about it. And also, when people are driving they see them. I think it kind of makes me, like, be careful. I think, okay, someone died there and it's kind of dangerous. Because I know there's one . . . down Manchaca, that two girls had just gotten their drivers' licenses. And there was, like, a curve and they wrecked because she was trying to change the radio station at the same time as she was driving. And, whenever I go around that curve now I'm really careful." Further, Maegan believes that newer drivers—as opposed to cyclists, more experienced motorists, or people who travel mainly by public transport—pay more attention to roadside crosses, especially those memorializing young people.

The crosses also denote dangerous driving conditions or topographical features. In addition to crosses, one student recalled seeing actual "warning signs done by the mom, dad, or friend," while another wrote, "I'm a little more cautious at these intersections and curves, I also tend to avoid them because I realize they are dangerous." Here the crosses are read as overtly cautionary.

Diversion

While serving as stark advisories, roadside crosses simultaneously provide a somewhat paradoxical diversion from the tedium of routine travel, provoking a range of emotive responses from compassion to anger. Not surprisingly, many informants reported feeling sad at the sight of a cross by the road. Others noted sympathy for those dealing with a sudden death. Hannah Day wrote, "I tend to wonder what happened, who it was—did I ever see them in the store or did they wait on me in a restaurant?" Like several other respondents, Hannah speculates about the people represented by the crosses.

For a number of students, the crosses and the deaths they signify stimulate perhaps their first thoughts about the nature of death and their own mortality, as the person who wrote, "It gives me a weird feeling to think that at one time someone died right there, and now everyone just goes on with their business like nothing ever happened." Similarly, another respondent was "sad, gloomy" to "realize that everyone is going on happily living while everyone who knew the person [who died] in the accident is dying inside."

One student recounted seeing someone at the cross on Stassney Lane, "I saw this grown man kneeling next to the flowers and the toys, and he was crying. It was raining hard but he stayed there crying and he put a new toy down and left. My heart went out to him and the little boy that died." While many students expressed similarly empathetic feelings toward the family and friends of the deceased, one woman, who had recently lost three friends in two separate accidents, wrote that she also feels sad for the "person(s) who made the accident happen" upon seeing a cross.

Another young woman stated, "If I see them, it kind of scares me. It could have been me just as easily. A lot of them were my age," while another responded that "It makes me wonder if that could ever happen to me or someone I love." Still another student stated that seeing them caused her to realize that she was lucky to be alive.

The reactions of individuals who have lost a friend or family member also involve memories of the accident or of their deceased loved one. "Sometimes I get sad and sometimes I get angry and other times I feel happy 'cause that is how I can remember people and also it makes me think about my life and that I don't want to die in an accident." Following the death of her boyfriend's brother in an auto accident, one woman stated that every time she sees a roadside cross, she is reminded of him. A student who witnessed the accident that killed Jacorey Williams wrote that upon seeing Jacorey's cross, s/he sometimes cries. Another witness, describing her reaction, stated, "I get a flashback of seeing his little body laying in the middle of the road. I remember the sadness that I felt and that my classmates felt as we stood ten feet from them [emergency medical technicians] working on him." In a moment, the crosses transport viewers from the mundane to the numinous through tangible memory.

Economic Integration and Social Levelling

The memorial aesthetic reflects economic integration and social levelling in both the decorative choices of assemblage construction and maintenance of the site. Whereas a cemetery may display an array of construction and decorative materials, from crudely fashioned crosses and plaques to elaborately detailed granite headstones, the range of materials utilized in the construction of roadside crosses is generally limited to wood and metal. Objects commonly left at these memorial sites—artificial flowers, rosaries, Lion King figurines, wreaths—are inexpensive and easily obtained. Photographs and notes are simply but effectively protected against the elements by plastic baggies or sheaths purchased from supermarkets or drug stores. Stones found nearby help anchor the cross, or form a border. Thus, affluence is not essential to the erection of an eye-catching or appreciated memorial, nor is impoverishment an impediment.

Moreover, the egalitarian nature of the memorials, and indeed of vehicular travel in general (McLuhan 1964, 197-200), remind viewers that everyone, regardless of income or status, inevitably faces death, often unexpectedly. The tributes speak to the human condition, and provoke community response. Family and friends often combine their efforts in constructing and maintaining the assemblages, as in the case of the memorials discussed in the previous chapter. Individuals who witnessed the accident, but did not know the deceased may contribute as well. These public memorial sites, in which the sacred and the secular come together, provide a singular opportunity for social grieving independent of class or cultural strictures, and the collective confrontation of violence and tragedy.

Folklore, Functionalism and Counterhegemony

Although not one of the oft-cited four functions of folklore, the practice of incorporating aspects of traditional culture in efforts toward social change is not new. Past scholarship has focused on the use of folksong by unions and other organized movements, e.g., John Greenway's seminal *American Folksongs of Protest*, first published in 1953. Greenway presents the songs of textile workers, abolitionists, miners, and other formal groups, stating that "labor has used established songs from the earliest times to carry its protest, and in so doing continues in a tradition that is as old as English folksong itself" (13).[5] In a 1966 issue of the *Journal of American Folklore*, R. Serge Denisoff, quoting Terence Qualter, details the similar efforts of singers of "propaganda songs" to "'recruit supporters, arouse sympathy, to counteract the feelings of despair, to encourage or inspire with hope for a new and happier future'" (582-83).[6]

The creation of the AIDS quilt, and quilting in general, represents a similar use of folklore, and specifically material culture (Lewis and Fraser 1996; Hawkins 1995). In the nineteenth century, quilts afforded women, who had no voice in the political sphere, a way to communicate socially critical sentiment. Examples of politically meaningful quilt patterns include the Radical Rose, the Drunkard's Path, and the Underground Railroad. The Radical Rose, for example, which was "popular in the North during the Civil War, had a black center for each flower and was a wordless statement of sympathy for the slaves" (Hawkins 1995, 771). Today, the AIDS quilt, which Lewis and Fraser call "the largest piece of folk art ever created," is a political tool as well a statement of profound grief and loss (1996, 434, 448).

Several factors unite uses made of customary folklife in protest song, AIDS-related projects, and social protest utilizing roadside crosses: the use of symbols with currency in a certain community, dynamic meaning behind the symbols, their connections to shared rites of passage (Van Gennep 1960), and the counter-hegemonic nature of the collective statement. Linked to traditional symbolism and customs surrounding death, political uses of vernacular expression acquire meaning and forcefulness.

Contemporary Halloween activities, for example, employ jack-o-lanterns, witches and skeletons—figures associated with liminality and death—as "personal statements made in a participatory group or community situation, using culturally valued and shared symbols, most of which are centuries old" (Santino 1983, 2). Likewise, as detailed in chapter two, the custom of marking a burial site with a cross is widespread in the Americas, as well having a long history in Europe. The roadside crosses, imbued with at least four hundred years of shared relevancy, tell basically the same story now as they did in the newly-colonized Mexico of the mid-sixteenth century. As Jennifer Solter stated, explaining the rationale behind MADD's choice of the cross as a communicative symbol, "the cross would call attention to a death . . . There wasn't just an injury, but they actually had a death." Although passers-by may speculate as to the particulars of an automobile accident, the fact of a death is sure. Further, the cross may be interpreted as something of an appeal to God, as in the custom of embroidering the letters "I.H.S." on a religious habit intended for burial use—the initials representing the Latin phrase *In Hoc Signo*, or "'In This Sign,' (i.e., the sign of the cross) . . . a visual means of commending oneself to the mercy of Christ" (Buckley and Cartwright 1983, 13). In Roman Catholic belief, a sudden death requires such a commendation, as the individual has died without the benefit of last rites. As a sacred symbol appearing in the highly public and profane realm of the road, the cross is denotative of mediation, and thus liminality. Folklorist Gary Butler notes that "when a death occurs, the sacred enters into uncomfortable contact with the profane and is embodied in the deceased, who is suddenly neither profane nor sacred" (1982, 31). The cross is indexic not only of death, but of the deceased as well, and renders the loss that of the entire community (Hawkins 1995, 757).

Employed as a tactic for incorporating a particular death into the consciousness of a community, a roadside cross actively confronts "the bureaucratization, specialization and compartmentalization of modern death," (Narváez 1994, 289-90)[7] another aspect of its counter-hegemonic capacity. Commuters pass crosses on major city and county thoroughfares at least twice a day. The memorialized death is not easily set aside after the funeral and burial, but remains a fixture of daily life. The tension between private grief and public rage is embodied in the memorial cross. It not only represents a death, but in the case of the MADD campaign, an organized, political movement and sentiment—drunk driving causes deaths. Austin resident Thomas Vannatta proposed a roadside memorial cross program to the Texas Highway Department in the early 1990s, the message similarly cautionary; he "envisioned the crosses as warnings to slow down," as well as a "comfort to the dead and their loved ones." It seems only appropriate that such communication take place in the arena of city and county roadways; the symbolism of death and tragedy, and the hope for rebirth of some kind, moving from the privacy of church and cemetery to the street. As with the stark listing of names on black granite that constitutes the Vietnam Veterans Memorial, contrasting with the more traditional war memorial imagery of glorious, triumphant aggression, viewers find themselves face-to-face with the reality of death.

The negotiation of death necessarily involves one's beliefs about life, and the expression of these beliefs is the complex result of conflicting forces (Primiano 1995, 43-45). While the particular message of a roadside cross is currently in flux, so too is that of the cross itself, both in the expressive behaviour of which it is a part, and in society at large. The use of the icon in popular culture, which incorporates Christian symbolism without obligation to the religious tenets usually accompanying it, is similar to its place in American civil religion. Crosses have long been a staple of popular fashion, from the punk (anti-)aesthetic born in 1970s England to current Celtic and Gothic chic, not to mention Catholic kitsch.[8] As Jenny Stinson told me, "Crosses aren't strictly religious anymore. Everybody wears them, whether they're Christians or not." The ambiguity and vigor of cross symbolism affords it a broad spectrum of meaning and importance in contemporary society.

The dynamism of publicly negotiated meaning mirrors the processes of separation and incorporation that grieving individuals must navigate. The liminal state of the individual, family or social group brought on by death confers special status upon them (Buckley and Cartwright 1983, 8-10), and perhaps renders their actions more influential. However, whereas death customs such as those found in wake tradition provide a mechanism for both separation and incorporation, the custom of marking the site of a fatal accident with a cross renders the death, in a sense, permanently betwixt and between. At Halloween, "death and randomness are incorporated into family stability and routine through home decorations," while "the street seems to be the arena for the airing of more topical fears . . . but the dread of the unknown and the uncontrollable continue to be addressed in both cases" (Santino 1983, 18). By focusing ongoing political activity on a public, tragic event and site, an individual simultaneously incorporates, yet refuses to passively accept, their sudden loss.

Several people I spoke with indicated puzzlement about the desire to construct such a public memorial. Tom Hurt, at the Texas Department of Transportation, said he would definitely *not* want a visible reminder of fatal accident involving a family member, even if its purpose was to make a political statement. Even those choosing to memorialize a death with a cross experience difficulty with its public nature. Solter said, "at first it really bothered me to go through the intersection. In fact, it took me several years to be able to go near William Cannon and Manchaca [a major intersection near the accident site]." The permanent liminality of roadside memorialization represents a counter-hegemonic approach to the contemporary "paucity of ritualistic conventions in the mourning period," as well as the authority of civil culture (Blauner 1977, 174-209). Further, deaths caused by drunk driving or carelessness contradict the perceived natural order of the life cycle. Here, institutional religion's assertion of "cosmological unity of life and death through the immortality of the soul" can be of little comfort (Narváez 1994, 285). Accordingly, many memorial participants do not identify the roadside crosses with any codified religion, but have integrated them into their vernacular religious practice, as they have incorporated the deaths they memorialize into their daily lives.

Solter visits Sara's cross, and her burial site, at least three times a year—on Christmas Day, Easter Sunday, and Sara's birthday (20 October), leaving flowers at both locations. When other family members pass by the cross, they make sure there is at least one bunch of flowers present. While his political efforts were not as successful as he had hoped, Thomas Vannatta continues to honor the memory of the young woman whose accident he witnessed by warning other drivers of dangerous road conditions. "I flash lights and signal with the universal slow down arm out the window when some large hazard looms," he wrote.

Vannatta's concern for public safety was deepened following a collision in which he was seriously injured. Death statistics are not publicized as they were in the fifties, sixties, and seventies, he observes, except on "dangerous" holidays such as Labor Day and New Year's Eve. Attributing it to ill-conceived changes in public policy, he writes, "Highway safety awareness has fallen to the wayside and has been replaced by an internal reliance on automotive engineering—a faulty hope. So I theorize that the public has taken the problem of warning and memorializing into their own hands. Often, as in my accident and after $25,000 in medical expenses and endless pain and treatment, there is no justice."

Jennifer stated that at the time she put up Sara's cross, the MADD members in Texas believed that a forceful public statement was necessary to combat the perception that drinking and driving was acceptable, and the tendency to blame fatal incidents on minority populations. She advocated the passage of legislation that would make Texas roads safer, and she feels that this helped her work through her loss: "Because when I went to change the laws and we lobbied, you know, for the first DWI law, and when we passed the first DWI law in fifty years, you know, I mean I felt like, that we really have accomplished something and I was doing something good out of something bad that had happened to me. And when I stood with other victims, you know, it made me feel stronger and that I couldn't feel sorry for myself because I understood there were other mothers hurting as much as I was." In uniting with other victims of drunk driving—an act made material by the construction and maintenance of Sara's memorial cross—Solter found solace and renewed strength.

Solter concluded that "if those few crosses out there have made the difference, you know, for MADD, I think we did make our statement." Just as the AIDS quilt's "provocative appearance on the [Washington] Mall gave the project's leadership an opportunity to denounce the country's indifference to the AIDS epidemic and to rally for greater attention to research and support" (Hawkins 1995, 759-60), the MADD crosses, and roadside crosses in general, are a counter-hegemonic grassroots cry for greater attention to safe roadway travel and harsher penalties for vehicular carelessness and crime. As Vannatta notes, "the crosses are also an expression of the frustration people have with the justice system. People cannot simply let go of traumatic life changing events that easily." As powerfully positioned mediators of beliefs about life and death, the crosses inhabit an equally unique position between private and public spheres of conformity and protest.

While the cross is an ancient symbol with centuries of accrued meaning, it is also a dynamic reflection of grief, hope and guidance to a measureless audience. Victor Turner has written that, "Liminality, marginality, and structural inferiority are conditions in which are frequently generated myths, symbols, rituals, philosophical systems, and works of art . . . Each of these productions has a multivocal character, having many meanings, and each is capable of moving people at many psychobiological levels simultaneously" ([1969] 1995, 128-29). The crosses occupy a unique place in Austin's urban landscape, especially those that are extralegal (not erected through MADD or the Texas Department of Highways). Their continued existence and increasing appearance are highly-charged reminders of the dangers of vehicular travel, stricter driving regulations and technological advances in automobiles and roadway construction notwithstanding.

In agreement with the popular feminist maxim "the personal *is* political," a number of Austin residents have attempted to use the memorial custom of the roadside cross to help prevent further tragedy, communicating with a largely unknown audience through the shared meaning of an universal sign. Political intent, rather than locating the roadside cross outside the realm of vernacular expression, confirms the objects' informal communicative power, especially among members of diverse community groups. As noted above, for viewers of the crosses—Austin motorists and other travelers—such distinctions between manifest meanings are often not consciously made, or are irrelevant. Finally, while such crosses and their attendant assemblages often represent a community's perception of the deceased individual, others have specifically chosen roadside crosses—like protesters have utilized vernacular song and AIDS activists have stitched quilt blocks—as active symbols of their hope for the future as well, and for their desire to prevent any further loss and suffering akin to their own.

Between Incorporation and Conflict

The examples cited here, however, should not be interpreted as indications of total acceptance or even familiarity with the custom throughout the area's populace, further underscoring the practice's interstitiality. One of my informants, a computer programmer in her late twenties, voiced strong opposition to the use of any religious symbolism in such a manner. As a clear violation of church and state, she believes that no religious symbol is appropriate to a public memorial. Similarly, the Oregon American Civil Liberties Union protested a senator's efforts to legalize roadside crosses in that state in early 2000 (Courcey 2000). During a 1997 interview, Texas Department of Transportation spokesperson Hurt asserted that to be fair, the state should either allow the display of any religious symbol, including the Star of David and the crescent moon, or none at all. He noted further that his office had received complaints about the religious overtones of roadside crosses. In February of 1998, Hurt informed me that the department had issued revised guidelines for the MADD markers which stated that "markers may be various types of symbols."

Several student respondents wrote that they had never seen or heard of objects by the side of the road marking the site of a fatal accident, in spite of the fact that there have been a number of memorial assemblages within yards of the school grounds. Thus one student stated that she had only *heard* of them, and described them as "yellow tape saying 'Do not cross' cones around the incident, etc."

Others perceive the phenomenon to be a primarily rural one, although certain areas of the city, as noted in chapter three, are home to several crosses. One respondent wrote, "Most of them are out in the country—or at least the suburbs, and since I don't leave the urban center of Austin, I don't see them too often." Similarly, another said "I've seen more of these crosses in desolate areas of wide open Texas roads than in heavily maintained and heavily signed areas of cities." An amateur cyclist did not recall seeing any crosses on Southwest Parkway, a highway he travels often by bicycle, and home to at least two roadside crosses.

Urban planner John Hickman expressed disbelief when I told him that Austin area residents were familiar with the custom. In the development of area land for projects ranging from city bus stop shelters to downtown strip malls, Hickman added, contractors and sub-contractors must consult City of Austin manuals. None of the manuals, to the best of his knowledge, included guidelines pertaining to roadside crosses (MADD-related or otherwise) or other vernacular memorials.

The fact that roadside crosses do not register on the cognitive maps of all area residents, or civic and county site maps, further highlights their informality and liminal status. Adding to the outlaw quality of the markers has been the absence of concrete guidelines for governmental entities in many areas, including central Texas. The city of Austin, for example, has a graffiti hotline which residents may call to report tagging and thus hasten its removal. Crosses, while occupying similar space in the city landscape, communicate in a less obscure and thus less threatening manner. It is difficult for city, county, and state officials to condemn emotionally charged objects that might encourage motorists to slow down, be more alert, or think twice before driving while intoxicated. It is perhaps equally easy to ignore them—as the student who wrote "I try not to look"—or become immune to them as have a number of other informants. Further, the markers represent an active locus for troublesome questions about the ever-present risks of injury and death in contemporary society. A questionnaire respondent poignantly expressed a sentiment with which perhaps all informants would agree, regardless of religious or political stance. Upon seeing a roadside cross, she feels sad and, she wrote, "[I] hope I don't see any more."

The assemblages may be distracting, and are certainly difficult to mow or build around. Nevertheless, city and state employees have been sensitive to their importance to families and communities, for which they are to be recognized and commended.[9] While the public display of religious symbolism, not to mention the manifestation of intense emotion, creates problems of policy and enforcement which may ultimately affect or prohibit their existence in the future, recent circumstances have allowed area residents much-needed creative space betwixt and between regulation and reality, past and present, public and private, sacred and profane.

Roadside memorials are polysemic manifestations of a number of cultural threads, a transient, vernacular art form crossing religious, cultural, and class lines both in rural areas and in increasingly congested urban environments. The manner in which such threads come together can be traced through the perceptions of area residents who make, decorate, maintain, and view the assemblages. Like formal tragedy and war memorials, vernacular memorials attempt to acknowledge and commemorate the unthinkable, as well as to address significantly different perceptions of the past and the present. Here, too, are struggles between the vernacular and the governmentally sanctioned—the private and public interpretation of tragic and sometimes criminal events. While the memorial sites analyzed here are not municipally constructed memorials, nor locations at which formal ceremonies have taken place, they are faithfully attended with a mixture of grief, reverence, and hope. Markedly different from the urban manifestations that surround them, they are treated accordingly by city, county, and state officials, as well as the community at large.

The cross, a powerful signifier, communicates on a number of levels as evidenced by informant response. The symbol's semiotic versatility allows the memorial sites to function as regenerative manifestations of both vernacular religion and grief work. Whereas contemporary funeral custom and landscape emphasize the difference between the deceased and those who mourn, roadside cross memorials present a more universally active, and thus affective, threshold.

Notes

Chapter One

1. For detailed studies of memorials and other public mourning for Diana in the UK and elsewhere, see Kear and Steinberg 1999; Wood 1998; Walter 1999; Walter and Biddle 1998.

2. An example of obliteration, followed years later by rectification, has taken place at the former site of Mount Cashel Orphanage in St. John's, Newfoundland. Following the trials that led to the convictions of several Christian brothers on counts of sexual and physical assault in 1989, the orphanage was closed. The buildings were razed in 1992 (Bates 1993). All that remained were several gateposts, painted grey and emblazoned with the Irish cross. In 1997, the land was purchased for the construction of a Sobey's grocery store. In June of 1998, small floral wreaths appeared atop the two main gateposts. Presently, the relocated gateposts are part of a small memorial area, along with a park bench and flower beds, located at the entrance to the shopping center and adjacent subdivision.

3. Johnson's memorial was painted over by unknown persons in early 2001 (Osborne 2001). Johnson's mother, Mary Boyd, who painted the mural in 1989, has since repainted it.

4. Foote discusses this kind of informal, interstitial communication about death sites with particular regard to John Dillinger, Bonnie Parker, and Clyde Barrow (1997, 212).

5. For example, see Young's account of vandalism of a Holocaust memorial at San Francisco's Jewish Museum (1993, 317-19), and Foote's report of similar problems occurring at the Haymarket riot police monument in Chicago (1997, 138-41).

6. While the Turners, as well as Pechilis, focus on established, conventional religious pilgrimage, Marion Bowman discusses New Age pilgrims as well as Christian visitors to Glastonbury. David Hufford's writing here is concerned with pilgrims to St. Anne de Beaupré in Québec.

Chapter Two

1. Atom Egoyan's film version of the book, released in 1997, is set in the Canadian province of British Columbia. No crosses appear in the film.

2. Executed on February 17, 1938 for a crime he did not commit, Juan is now venerated for his ability to aid in the eradication of illness

and for other miracles that have occurred in the area. The shrine incorporates his grave and execution site, marked by several crosses, and a chapel (Griffith 1987, 75-80).

3. Benson also cites observance of the commandment regarding graven images (Exodus 20:4), and the efforts of early Christians to conceal their faith from the Romans as obstacles to the adoption of the cross as a positive symbol (40).

4. The expression of civil religion is, of course, often problematic. Folklorist Sue Samuelson describes a court case in which she was an expert witness for the defense. In December, 1979, the city of Denver, Colorado was sued by a group called Citizens Concerned for the Separation of Church and State, with the support of the American Civil Liberties Union. They charged that a nativity scene on the steps of the city hall was a "religious symbol which should not appear on government property" (1982, 139). The city won the case, and at the time of Samuelson's writing the citizens' group was appealing the decision.

Kugelmass cites Jonathan Woocher (1988) and Charles Silberman (1985) in the identification of American Jewish civil religion, which is often linked with the resurgence of Jewish nationalism resulting from the Six Day War (1994, 176-77). The conflict over religious symbolism at Auschwitz offers an example of a contested intersection of Jewish and (predominately) Christian civil religion on the international stage.

5. See McCarty, 1983.

6. California resident Candy Lightner founded Mothers Against Drunk Driving (MADD) in 1980—a response to her frustrating experience with the justice system following the death of her thirteen-year-old daughter in a drunk driving incident. Originally composed of all female members, the organization now includes people of any age or gender.

7. Woolf writes that MADD crosses are also approved for use in Louisiana, Ohio, and Florida. He further notes a similar highway safety program in Montana, not restricted to drunk driving deaths, where roadside crosses are erected by the American Legion.

8. Liungman observes that St. Andrew's cross (so-called because according to legend, out of humility Andrew refused to be executed on a cross identical to that on which Jesus Christ was crucified) predates Christianity and adorns prehistoric cave walls in Europe. Additionally, it was a figure in both early Chinese ideography (representing the number five) and Egyptian hieroglyphics (divide, count, and break into parts)

(1991, 139, 322). Coincidentally, crosses of this kind are routinely marked with pencil or red brick on two different structures believed to house the remains of New Orleans' alleged voodoo priestess Marie Laveau (Tallant 1983, 127, 129). Drawing the crosses is part of a ritual in which the visitor offers a wish or request.

9. Although unsure of the details, my father, an area resident, confirmed that a serious automobile accident in which at least three people were killed had recently occurred at the site.

Chapter Three

1. In the mid-1980s the road was thick with small white crosses. It now appears that the majority of these have been removed as a result of on-going highway repair and improvement projects. Correspondingly, both Foote and Henzel attribute the absence of crosses on stretches of road known to be deadly as indicative of government intervention (Foote 1997, 171-2; Henzel 1991, 97-8).

2. This statement on the cross may be based on an oft-quoted line among "Star Trek" fans from the 1982 motion picture *Star Trek II-The Wrath of Khan*. A dying Spock utters the words to his long-time friend, James Kirk.

3. A dreamcatcher is an artifact of Native American origin consisting of a hoop encircling a web of, for example, wool or twine decorated with beads, crystals, or feathers. Hung above one's bed, the dreamcatcher captures bad dreams while allowing good dreams to pass through.

4. One of Tara's favorite movies was *The Lion King*, and she collected snow globes.

5. Gerald Pocius also notes differences between Catholic and Protestant iconography in home decoration (1986, 125). Of particular significance to the present discussion is his reference to the popularity of angels in Protestant popular prints (147). Leonard Primiano discusses the recent upsurge in this popularity in "Angels and Americans," 1998. Angel figurines are frequently left at Austin's memorial sites, including cemeteries. For a discussion of the historical use of angel imagery and cemetery statuary, see McDannell 1995, 125-127.

6. Although leaving a stone at a roadside memorial coincides with Catholic Mexican and Mexican-American custom as documented in Mexico, Arizona, etc., most stones and rocks present at memorials in the Austin area appeared to be decorative (e.g., spelling out initials or forming a border around the assemblage) or meant to stabilize the cross.

At only one cross (Fig. 3.6), did the rocks not appear to be decorative *or* supportive.

7. While I did find car parts at the memorials, I did not observe any that were incorporated into the structure of the cross itself, as reported by Arrellano (1986, 42).

8. While the data presented here does not lend itself to an examination of floral symbolism, the topic is certainly integral to death custom (see, e.g., Carmichael and Sayer 1991, 16-21; Drury 1994; Goody 1993; Walter 1990). The red rose, for example, has long been understood as symbolic of martyrdom, as in the annual commemoration of the fourteen female victims of the 1989 Montréal Massacre.

Chapter Four

1. See, for example, the work of Olivia Cadaval (1985) on the Day of the Dead celebrations in Washington, D.C.; James Griffith's (1992) observations of both Mexican-American and O'Odham customs in southern Arizona; and Kay Turner and Pat Jasper (1994) with regard to the custom in south Texas, particularly its economic aspects.

2. For related studies, see Sciorra, 1993, concerning Our Lady of Mount Carmel Grotto in Rosebank, Staten Island, and Cooper and Sciorra, 1994, documenting memorial murals in New York City.

3. Tammy's parents and Nathan's mother are the primary caretakers of the memorial for the three teenagers. Jeff's mother, to whom Susan refers here, has not been involved.

4. Grief work, as described by Jack Kamerman, involves the expression of grief facilitating a return to normal levels of functioning and may include, for culturally variable periods of time, "*bodily distress, a preoccupation with the image of the deceased, guilt, hostility,* and *alteration or loss of normal patterns of conduct*" [emphasis in original]. Although grief work is necessarily "painful and difficult," failure to work through bereavement may result in severe, and sometimes pathological, grief reactions (1988, 66-7).

5. For a closer examination of the relationship between roadside memorials and corresponding burial sites, including those discussed in this chapter, see Everett 2000. J. Joseph Edgette (1997) has explored such connections between a number of sites in Pennsylvania.

6. Here Vicki refers to "homecoming mums," large, elaborately decorated chrysanthemums traditionally worn by women to high school homecoming football games. The Cavalettes is the school's dance team,

of which Tara was a proud member. Taking the mum "as a keepsake" might be interpreted as a variation on the idea of the "linking object" introduced by psychiatrist Vamik Volkan (1972, 215-221) and further developed by, for example, Worden (1991, 84-86) and Silverman and Nickman (1996, 81). Here, the linking object is not a former possession of the deceased, but has been indelibly associated with her by its placement at the cross.

7. In addition, because of the transience of such memorials, speedy documentation by folklorists is imperative. The memorial for Heather Lamay and Lisa Wendenburg is already gone, and that for Tammy, Nathan, and Jeff has seen at least four incarnations. As noted above, Kwolek-Folland's call for vernacular architecture studies to consider transient, as well as permanent characteristics of vernacular structures, is certainly applicable here.

8. See Pocius, 2001, for a similar discussion of grave decoration in Newfoundland, with particular emphasis on the importance of distinguishing between wilderness and culture in ritual decorative practice.

9. See also Kay Turner's discussion of women's home altars in this regard (1999, 83-89).

Chapter Five

1. Functionalism does not adequately account for social conflict or change, but rather, resulting from its origins in the idea of socio-cultural evolution, embraces only those aspects of culture contributing to (re)integration (Doucette 1993, 132-33, Oring 1976, 67-80). See, for example Radner 1993, and Greenhill and Tye 1997, for essays concerning the subversive in traditional culture.

2. I decided to focus on students at Crockett High School, in south Austin, for several reasons. Firstly, as an alumnus of the school, I was able to work with a former teacher of mine and make a connection with the participating students on the basis of shared experience. Secondly, Crockett is located in an area of the city in which there are a number of roadside crosses, not the least of which was across the street from the school (the memorial for Jacorey Williams, Fig. 3.14). Thirdly, the school is attended by a mix of students, from different ethnic and economic backgrounds, that loosely mirrors the city's larger population. While given an option to include their names and phone numbers if they were interested in speaking with me privately, participants were not required to include any personal information.

3. As previously noted, however, acts of vandalism have occurred. The site on Guadalupe street maintained by Susan Crane and Margie Franklin has been disturbed more than once. The crosses memorializing Daniel London and Beth Early (Fig. 3.4-5) were stolen, along with the flowers left at the site, in June of 1999 (Banta 1999).

4. The "memorial libation" is an ancient memorial ritual with a long pedigree in African and African diaspora cultures (see, e.g., Cooper and Sciorra 1994, 77; Georgia Writers' Project 1940, 59, 114, 237-38).

5. Greenway relates further :

William of Malmesbury, writing in the early twelfth century, tells of his ancient predecessor, Aldhelm, standing beside a bridge, singing secular ditties until he had gained the attention of passers-by, when he gradually began to introduce religious ideas into his songs. Twelve hundred years later Jack Walsh, who had never heard of Aldhelm or his biographer, posted his Wobbly band beside a highway and sang religious songs until he had gained the attention of passers-by, when he gradually began to introduce secular ideas into his songs (1960, 13).

6. Quotation from Terence H. Qualter's *Propaganda and Psychological Warfare* (New York: Random House) in Denisoff 1966.

7. See also Buckley and Cartwright 1983, 13.

8. I use "kitsch" here, as does Primiano, to indicate "affection and joy at the absurd or outrageous aspects of the ethnic, regional, and national [material] expressions of the [Catholic] tradition" (1999, 198). For another discussion of popular usages of Catholic iconography, see Cosentino 1996.

9. In the past, road maintenance crew members have routinely refused to disturb the assemblages.

Bibliography

16-year-old Luling boy killed in 1-car wreck. 1996. *Austin American-Statesman*, 26 February, http://archives.statesman.com

Anti-abortion crosses burned by vandals at Baptist church. 1998. *Austin American-Statesman*, 18 January, http://archives.statesman.com

Arrellano, Estevan. 1986. Descansos. *New Mexico Magazine*, February, 42-44.

Armstrong, Robert Plant. 1981. *The Powers of Presence: Consciousness, Myth, and Affecting Presence.* Philadelphia: University of Pennsylvania Press.

Aulén, Gustaf. 1970. *The Drama and the Symbols.* Trans. Sydney Linton. London: S.P.C.K.

Austin man charged in stabbing death. 1996. *Austin American-Statesman*, 8 June, http://archives.statesman.com

Austinite is killed while fleeing wreck, police say. 1996. *Austin American-Statesman*, 5 May, http://archives.statesman.com

Babineck, Mark. 1997. Builder expects "ads for Jesus" to multiply. *Austin American-Statesman*, 18 July, http://archives.statesman.com

Banks, Russell. 1991. *The Sweet Hereafter.* Toronto: McClelland & Stewart.

Banta, Bob. 1999. Vandalism renews families' suffering. *Austin American-Statesman*, 7 June. B1, 3.

Barber, Paul. 1988. *Vampires, Burial and Death: Folklore and Reality.* New Haven, CT: Yale University Press.

Barrera, Alberto. 1991. Mexican-American Roadside Crosses in Starr County. In *Hecho en Tejas: Texas-Mexican Folk Arts and Crafts*, ed. Joe S. Graham, 278-92. Publications of the Texas Folklore Society. 50. Denton: University of North Texas Press.

Bartoszewski, Wladyslaw T. 1991. *The Convent at Auschwitz.* New York: George Braziller.

Bascom, William R. 1954. Four Functions of Folklore. *Journal of American Folklore* 67: 333-49.

Bates, Allison. 1993. S.v. "orphanages." *Encyclopedia of Newfoundland and Labrador.*

Bellah, Robert. 1990. Civil Religion in America. In *Culture and Society: Contemporary Debates*, ed. by Jeffrey C. Alexander and Steven Seidman, 262-272. Cambridge: Cambridge University Press.

Benson, George Willard. 1976. *The Cross: Its History and Symbolism.* New York: Hacker Art Book.

Berlandier, Jean Louis. 1980. *Journey to Mexico During the Years 1826-1834.* Trans. Sheila M. Ohlendorf, et. al. 2 vols. Austin: Texas State Historical Association.

Biggs, Vicki. 1998. Interview by author. Austin, Texas, 15 January.

Blauner, Richard. 1977. Death and Social Structure. *Passing: The Vision of Death in America,* ed. Charles O. Jackson, 174-209. Contributions in Family Studies, Number 2. Westport, CT: Greenwood Press.

—— Bodnar, John. 1992. *Remaking America: Public Memory, Commemoration, and Patriotism in the Twentieth Century.* Princeton: Princeton University Press.

Bosque, Fernando del. [1908] 1963. Diary of Fernando Del Bosque, 1675. In *Spanish Exploration in the Southwest 1542-1706,* ed. H. E. Bolton, 291-309. Trans. H. E. Bolton. New York: Barnes & Noble.

Bowie High student, 17, dies after Slaughter Lane wreck. 1997. *Austin American-Statesman* 11 May, http://archives.statesman.com

Bowman, Marion. 1993. Drawn to Glastonbury. In *Pilgrimage in Popular Culture,* ed. Ian Reader and Tony Walter, 29-62. London: Macmillan.

Boyd, Linda. 1997. Personal communication with author. Austin, Texas, 5 May.

Britton, Ryan. 1998. E-mail to the author. 18 March.

Buckley, Anna-Kaye and Christina Cartwright. 1983. The Good Wake: A Newfoundland Case Study. *Culture & Tradition* 7: 6-16.

Butler, Gary R. 1982. Sacred and Profane Space: Ritual Interaction and Process in the Newfoundland House Wake. *Material History Bulletin* 15: 27-32.

Cadaval, Olivia. 1985. "The Taking of the Renwick": The Celebration of the Day of the Dead and the Latino Community of Washington, D.C. *Journal of Folklore Research* 22: 179-84.

Canales, David. 1997. Personal communication with author. 26 April.

Cantú, Norma. 1991. Costume as Cultural Resistance and Affirmation: The Case of a South Texas Community. In *Hecho en Tejas: Texas-Mexican Folk Arts and Crafts,* ed. Joe S. Graham, 117-30. Publications of the Texas Folklore Society. 50. Denton: University of North Texas Press.

Carmichael, Elizabeth and Chloë Sayer. 1991. *The Skeleton at the Feast: The Day of the Dead in Mexico.* London: British Museum Press.

Carpentier, Paul. 1981. *Les croix de chemin: Au-dela du signe.* Ottawa: National Museums of Canada, National Museum of Man, Mercury Series.

Cement truck flips over, killing Austin man, 44: Motorcyclist, 43, dies in crash: Friday accident victim identified: South First traffic flow restricted: Alcohol ID sting nets 35 arrests: Vote on school. 1997. *Austin American-Statesman,* 14 September, http://archives. statesman.com

Charmaz, Kathy. 1980. *The Social Reality of Death.* Reading, MA: Addison-Wesley.

Cooper, Martha and Joseph Sciorra. 1994. *R.I.P.: New York Spraycan Memorials.* London: Thames and Hudson.

Cosentino, Donald. Madonna's Earrings: Catholic Icons as Ethnic Chic. 1996. *In Recycled, Re-seen: Folk Art from the Global Scrap Heap,* eds. Charlene Cerny and Suzanne Seriff, 166-79. New York: Harry N. Abrams.

Courcey, Kevin. 2000. Another Roadside Attraction. Corvallis Secular Society newsletter. February, http://css.peak.org/index.html

Crane, Susan. 1998. Telephone interview by author. 20 January.

Day, Don. 1998. Telephone interview by author. 20 January.

Day, Hannah. 1997. Response to "Accident Marker Questionnaire" administered by author. Austin, Texas, 12 May.

Dead motorcyclist identified. 1997. *Austin American-Statesman,* 28 September, http://archives.statesman.com

De León, Alonso. [1908] 1963. Itinerary of the De León Expedition of 1689. In *Spanish Exploration in the Southwest 1542-1706,* ed. H. E. Bolton, 388-404. Trans. Elizabeth Howard West. New York: Barnes & Noble.

Dedrick, Geraldine, Florence Dagle and Krista Dagle. 1998. Interview by Avril Benoit. *This Morning.* Canadian Broadcasting Corporation, Radio One, 2 February.

Delvecchio, Julie. 1997. Memorials may help the grieving, but road experts are divided. *Sydney [Australia] Morning Herald,* 23 June, http://www.smh.com.au/daily/content/970623/national/national13.html

Denisoff, R. Serge. 1966. Songs of Persuasion: A Sociological Analysis of Urban Propaganda Songs. *Journal of American Folklore* 79: 581-89.

DeWolf, Rose. 1996. The mourning after: Impromptu tributes make new tradition. *Houston Chronicle,* 7 September, Religion section, p. 1.

Dominguez de Mendoza, Juan. [1908] 1963. Itinerary of Juan Dominguez de Mendoza, 1684. In *Spanish Exploration in the Southwest 1542-1706*, ed. H. E. Bolton, 320-343. Trans. H. E. Bolton. New York: Barnes & Noble.

DOT Won't Install Roadside Crosses. 1998. Miami Office of the Anti-Defamation League, 31 January, http://www.adl.org/Regional/Miami/DOTWontInstallRoadsideCrosses.html

Doucette, Laurel. 1993. Voices Not Our Own. *Canadian Folklore Canadien* 15.2: 119-37.

Drury, Susan. 1994. Funeral Plants and Flowers in England: Some Examples. *Folklore* 105: 101-103.

Dwork, Debórah and Robert Jan van Pelt. 1994. Reclaiming Auschwitz. In *Holocaust Remembrance: The Shapes of Memory*, ed. Geoffrey H. Hartman, 232-51. Cambridge, MA: Blackwell.

Edgette, J. Joseph. 1997. Death Site and Grave Sites: Bridging the Memory. Paper read at American Folklore Society Annual Meeting, Austin, Texas.

Escobar, Mario. 1998. Personal communication with author. St. John's, Newfoundland, 21 May.

Everett, Gary. 1997. Personal communication with author. Conroe, Texas, 25 October.

Everett, Christie. 1997. Personal communication with author. Austin, Texas, 22 December.

Everett, Holly. 1998. Crossroads: Roadside accident memorials in and around Austin, Texas. Master's thesis, Memorial University of Newfoundland.

_____. 2000. Roadside Crosses and Memorial Complexes in Texas. *Folklore* 111: 91-103.

Fehrenbach, T.R. 2000. *Lone Star: A History of Texas and the Texans*. Boulder, CO: Da Capo Press.

Firth, Raymond. 1973. *Symbols: Public and Private*. Ithaca, NY: Cornell University Press.

Fish, Lydia. 1987. The Last Firebase. *International Folklore Review* 5: 82-86.

Fiske, John. 1982. *Introduction to Communication Studies*. New York: Methuen & Co.

— Foote, Kenneth. 1997. *Shadowed Ground: America's Landscapes of Violence and Tragedy*. Austin: University of Texas Press.

Franklin, Margie. 1998. Telephone interview by author. 12 January.

Friends reflect on life of teen who died. 1996. *Austin American-Statesman,* 29 June, http://archives.statesman.com

Georgia Writers' Project. 1940. *Drums and Shadows: Survival Studies Among the Georgia Coastal Negroes.* Athens, GA: University of Georgia Press.

Goldstein, Diane. 1997. E-mail to folklore@tamum1.tamu.edu, 22 January.

Goody, Jack. 1993. The Culture of Flowers. Cambridge: Cambridge University Press.

— Gopnik, Adam. 1997. Crazy Piety. *The New Yorker,* 29 September, 34-37.

Gorer, Geoffrey. 1965. *Death, Grief and Mourning.* Garden City, NY: Doubleday & Company.

Graham, Joe S., comp. 1989. *Hispanic-American Material Culture: An Annotated Directory of Collections, Sites, Archives, and Festivals in the United States.* New York: Greenwood Press.

_____. 1996. Mexican Americans. In *American Folklore: An Encyclopedia,* ed. Jan Harold Brunvand. New York: Garland.

Granados, Christine. 1993. UT student dies of head injuries in traffic accident: Wreck occurred at East 26th and Beanna streets. *Austin American-Statesman,* 25 November, http://archives.statesman.com

Greenhill, Pauline and Diane Tye, eds. 1997. *Undisciplined Women: Tradition and Culture in Canada.* Montreal: McGill-Queen's.

Greenway, John. 1960. *American Folksongs of Protest.* New York: A.S. Barnes and Company, Inc.

Grieg, Jane S. 1996. Reply to letter of S.C. *Austin American-Statesman,* 31 December, E1.

Grider, Sylvia. 2001. Preliminary Observations Regarding the Spontaneous Shrines Following the Terrorist Attacks of September 11, 2001. *New Directions in Folklore* 4.2. http://www.temple.edu/isllc/newfolk/shrines.html

Griffith, James S. 1987. El Tiradito and Juan Soldado: Two Victim Intercessors of the Western Borderlands. *International Folklore Review* 5: 75-81.

_____. 1992. *Beliefs and Holy Places: A Spiritual Geography of the Pimería Alta.* Tucson: University of Arizona Press.

Gundaker, Grey. 1994. Halloween Imagery in Two Southern Settings. In *Halloween and Other Festivals of Death and Life,* ed. Jack Santino, 247-66. Knoxville: University of Tennessee Press.

Hancock, Ian. 1997. Personal communication with author. Austin, Texas, 7 May.

Harmon, Dave. 1997. Cross symbolizes closure for family of teen who died. *Austin American-Statesman*, 12 May, B1, 4.

— Hass, Kristin Ann. 1998. *Carried to the Wall: American Memory and the Vietnam Veterans Memorial*. Berkeley: University of California Press.

Hawkins, Peter S. 1995. Naming Names: The Art of Memory and the NAMES Project AIDS Quilt. *Critical Inquiry* 19: 752-79.

Henry, Hugh T. 1925. *Catholic Customs and Symbols*. New York: Benziger Brothers.

Henzel, Cynthia. 1991. *Cruces* in the Roadside Landscape of Northeastern Mexico. *Journal of Cultural Geography* 11.2: 93-106.

Hickman, John. 1997. Telephone interview by author. 1 June.

Hollis, G. 1998. Roadside Memorial Cross. 5 June, http://www.netusa1.net/~ghollis/

Hoppe, Leigh and Christian R. Gonzalez. 1996. 2nd Bowie student dies of injuries from wreck. *Austin American-Statesman*, 15 January, http://archives.statesman.com

Hufford, David J. 1985. Ste. Anne de Beaupre: Roman Catholic Pilgrimage and Healing. *Western Folklore* 44: 194-207.

Hurt, John. 1997. Interview by author. Austin, Texas, 2 May.

Jordan, Terry. 1982. *Texas Graveyards*. Austin: University of Texas Press.

Jordan, Terry, and John L. Bean and William M. Holmes, Jr. 1984. *Texas, A Geography*. Boulder: Westview Press.

Jordan, Terry, and Lester Rowntree. 1990. *The Human Mosaic: A Thematic Introduction to Cultural Geography*. New York: Harper & Row.

Kamerman, Jack B. 1988. *Death in the Midst of Life*. Englewood Cliffs, NJ: Prentice Hall.

Kear, Adrian and Deborah Lynn Steinberg. 1999. *Mourning Diana: Nation, Culture and the Performance of Grief*. New York: Routledge.

Kelly, Carolyn. 1996. Car-truck collision takes two lives. *Austin American-Statesman*, 6 January, http://archives.statesman.com

Kozak, David and Camillus Lopez. 1991. The Tohono O'odham Shrine Complex: Memorializing the Location of Violent Death. *New York Folklore* 17.1-2: 1-20.

Kugelmass, Jack. 1994. Why We Go to Poland: Holocaust Tourism as Secular Ritual. In *The Art of Memory: Holocaust Memorials in History*, ed. James E. Young, 175-84. New York: Prestel.

Kwolek-Folland, Angela. 1995. Gender as a Category of Analysis in Vernacular Architecture Studies. In *Gender, Class and Shelter: Perspectives in Vernacular Architecture*, ed. Elizabeth Collins Cromley and Carter L. Hudgins, 3-10. Knoxville: University of Tennessee Press.

Laderman, Gary. 1996. *The Sacred Remains: American Attitudes Toward Death, 1799-1883*. New Haven: Yale University Press.

Lamay, Shilah. 1997. Interview by author. Austin, Texas, 21 May.

Lemieux, Josh. 1994. Family, friends gather to remember 21 students killed in Alton bus crash. *Austin-American Statesman,* 22 September, http://archives.statesman.com

Lewis, Jacqueline and Michael R. Fraser. 1996. Patches of Grief and Rage: Visitor Responses to the NAMES Project AIDS Memorial Quilt. *Qualitative Sociology* 19: 433-451.

Lindell, Chuck. 1992. 2 Austin High students killed after car goes out of control, hits pole. *Austin American-Statesman,* 1 October, http://archives.statesman.com

Liungman, Carl G. 1991. *Dictionary of Symbols.* Santa Barbara: ABC-Clio.

Mandelbaum, David. 1959. Social Uses of Funeral Rites. In *The Meaning of Death*, ed. Herman Feifel, 189-217. New York: McGraw-Hill.

Marshall, Thom. 1995. So many wrecks, so many crosses. *Houston Chronicle*, 16 April, A21.

Massenet, Damián. [1908] 1963. Letter of Fray Damián Massenet to Don Carlos de Sigüenza, 1690. In *Spanish Exploration in the Southwest 1542-1706*, ed. H. E. Bolton, 353-387. Trans. Lilia M. Casís. New York: Barnes & Noble.

McCarty, Kieran, trans. 1983. Translation of letter from Felipe de Neve to Pedro Corbalán. *Southwest Mission Research Center Newsletter*, 17.54: 7.

McComb, David G. 1989. *Texas: A Modern History.* Austin: University of Texas Press.

McDannell, Colleen. 1995. *Material Christianity: Religion and Popular Culture in America.* New Haven: Yale University Press.

McLuhan, Marshall. 1964. *Understanding Media.* Toronto: Signet.

McRee, Kathleen and Sam Larcombe. 1993. *Roadside Crosses of New Mexico.* Videocassette.

"Memorial Markers." 1998. Imago Multimedia's Home Page, 2 June, http://home1.gte.net/imago2/memorial.html

Milspaw, Yvonne. 1986. Protestant Home Shrines: Icon and Image. *New York Folklore* 12.3-4: 119-36.

Mitford, Jessica. 1963. *The American Way of Death*. London: Hutchinson & Co.

Monger, George. 1997. Modern Wayside Shrines. *Folklore* 108: 113-114.

Monroe, Nichole. 1996. Friends reflect on life of teen who died. *Austin American-Statesman*, 29 June, http://archives.statesman.com

———. 1997. Accidents near Giddings leave 2 dead, 5 injured: Those killed in crashes not wearing seat belts, officials say. *Austin American-Statesman*, 9 May, http://archives.statesman.com

Morinis, Alan. 1984. *Pilgrimage in the Hindu Tradition: A Case Study of West Bengal*. Delhi: Oxford University Press.

Narváez, Peter. 1994. "Tricks and Fun": Subversive Pleasures at Newfoundland Wakes. *Western Folklore* 53: 263-94.

Nichols, John. 1994. *The Milagro Beanfield War*. New York: Henry Holt and Co.

Nöth, Winfried. 1995. *Handbook of Semiotics*. Bloomington: Indiana University Press.

O'Brien, Mary. 1981. *The Politics of Reproduction*. London: Routledge & Kegan Paul.

Ohlendorf, Tom. 1997. Interview by author. Austin, Texas, 2 May.

Oring, Elliott. 1976. Three Functions of Folklore. *Journal of American Folklore* 89: 67-80.

Osborn, Claire. 1996. Parents raise safety issues after boy hit, killed by car: Parents take action after boy's death: Safety petition circulated after 8-year-old is killed by car after leaving bus. *Austin American-Statesman*, 18 October, http://archives.statesman.com

Osborne, Jonathan. 2001. Roadside tribute to dead son vanishes. *Austin American-Statesman*, 20 April.

Owens, Maida. 1998a. Louisiana Roadside Memorials: Patterns, Influences, and Distribution. Unpublished paper.

———. 1998b. Roadside Memorial Crosses in Louisiana. Paper read at American Folklore Society Annual Meeting, Eugene, Oregon.

Panourgiá, Neni. 1995. *Fragments of Death, Fables of Identity: An Athenian Anthropography*. Madison: University of Wisconsin Press.

Pechilis, Karen. 1992. To Pilgrimage It. *Journal of Ritual Studies* 6.2: 59-92.

Perlez, Jane. 1997. Religious Symbols' Removal Ends Auschwitz Dispute. *New York Times International*, 13 December.

Phillips, Jim. 1994. Yogurt killings lawsuit settled for $12 million. *Austin American-Statesman*, 11 January, http://archives.statesman.com

Pocius, Gerald. 1986. Holy Pictures in Newfoundland Houses. In *Media Sense: The Folklore-Popular Culture Continuum*, ed. Peter Narváez and Martin Laba, 124-48. Bowling Green, OH: Bowling Green State University Popular Press.

_____. 2001. Decorating the Grave in Newfoundland: Maintaining Borders, Blurring Categories. In *Entre Beauce et Acadie: Facettes d'un Parcours Ethnologique*, 338-350. Québec City: Les Presses de l'Université Laval.

Point, Michael. 1991. Vaughan anniversary to pass quietly: Most fans remember late bluesman in a personal way. *Austin American-Statesman*, 22 August, http://archives.statesman.com

Porter, Kevin. 2001. Debate rekindles on safety of roads. *The News Herald*, 30 May, http://www.newsherald.com/articles/2001/05/30/lo053001a.htm

Powell, Doug. 1998. Interview by author. Austin, Texas, 17 January.

Power, Susan. 1994. *The Grass Dancer*. London: Picador.

Primiano, Leonard. 1995. Vernacular Religion and the Search for Method in Religious Folklife. *Western Folklore* 54: 37-56.

_____. 1997. Personal communication with author. St. John's, Newfoundland, 9 August.

_____. 1998. On Angels and Americans. *America*, 10 October, 15-17.

_____. 1999. Postmodern Sites of Catholic Sacred Materiality. In *Perspectives on American Religion and Culture*, ed. Peter W. Williams, 187-202. Malden, MA: Blackwell Publishers.

Radner, Joan Newlon, ed. 1993. *Feminist Messages: Coding in Women's Folk Culture*. Urbana: University of Illinois Press.

Ramos, Mary G., ed. 1997. *1998-1999 Texas Almanac*. Dallas: Dallas Morning News.

Reader, Ian. 1993. Introduction. *Pilgrimage in Popular Culture*, ed. Ian Reader and Tony Walter, 1-25. London: Macmillan.

Reed, Raymond. Telephone interview. 18 June 1997.

Rees, Elizabeth. 1992. *Christian Symbols, Ancient Roots*. London: Jessica Kingsley.

Richardson, Ruth. 1993. Death's Door: Thresholds and Boundaries in British Funeral Customs. In *Boundaries and Thresholds: Papers from a Colloquium of The Katharine Briggs Club*, ed. Hilda Ellis Davidson, 91-102. Woodchester: Thimble Press.

Rosenblatt, Paul C., R. Patricia Walsh and Douglas A. Jackson. 1976. *Grief and Mourning in Cross-Cultural Perspective*. n.c.: HRAF Press.

Safanov, Anatol. 1948. Cemetery. *The Universal Jewish Encyclopedia*, ed. Isaac Landman, vol. 3 of 10. New York: Universal Jewish Encyclopedia.

Samuelson, Sue. 1982. Folklore and the Legal System: The Expert Witness. *Western Folklore* 41: 139-44.

Santino, Jack. 1983. Halloween in America. *Western Folklore* 42: 1-20.

Sellars, Richard West and Tony Walter. 1993. From Custer to Kent State: Heroes, Martyrs and the Evolution of Popular Shrines in the USA. In *Pilgrimage in Popular Culture*, ed. Ian Reader and Tony Walter, 179-200. London: Macmillan.

Sered, Susan. 1988. The Domestication of Religion: The Spiritual Guardianship of Elderly Jewish Women. *Man* 23.3: 506-21.

Sciorra, Joseph P. 1993. Multivocality and Vernacular Architecture: The Our Lady of Mount Carmel Grotto in Rosebank, Staten Island. In *Studies in Italian American Folklore*, ed. Luisa del Guidice, 203-243. Logan, Utah: Utah State University Press.

Silberman, Charles. 1985. *A Certain People: American Jews and Their Lives Today*. New York: Summit Books.

Silverman, Phyllis R. 1981. *Helping Women Cope With Grief*. London: Sage.

_____ and Steven L. Nickman. 1996. Children's Construction of Their Dead Parents. In *Continuing Bonds: New Understandings of Grief*, eds. Dennis Klass, Phyllis R. Silverman, and Steven L. Nickman, 73-86. Washington, DC: Taylor & Francis.

Simons, Helen and Cathryn A. Hoyt, eds. 1992. *A Guide to Hispanic Texas*. Austin: University of Texas Press.

Solter, Jennifer. 1997. Telephone interview by author. 2 June.

Sosebee, Trevor. Personal communication with author. Austin, Texas, 2 May.

Steinhart, Peter. 1983. Our Off-Road Fantasy. In *The Automobile and American Culture*, ed. David L. Lewis and Laurence Goldstein, 346-52 . Ann Arbor: University of Michigan Press.

Stinson, Jenny. 1997a. Response to "Accident Marker Questionnaire" administered by author. Austin, Texas, 12 May.

_____. 1997b. Telephone interview by author. 14 May.

Tallant, Robert. [1946] 1983. *Voodoo in New Orleans*. Gretna, LA: Pelican.

Taylor, Richard P. 2000. *Death and the Afterlife: A Cultural Encyclopedia*. Denver: ABC-Clio.

Thatcher, Rebecca. 1995. Teen in fatal car wreck is remembered with cross. *Austin American-Statesman*, 4 May, http://archives. statesman.com

Tuan, Yi Fu. 1978. Sacred Space: Explorations of an Idea. In *Dimensions of Human Geography*, ed. Karl W. Butzer, 84-99. University of Chicago Department of Geography Research Paper. 186.

Turner, Kay. 1999. *Beautiful Necessity: The Art and Meaning of Women's Altars*. New York, Thames and Hudson.

Turner, Kay and Pat Jasper. 1994. Day of the Dead: The Tex-Mex Tradition. In *Halloween and Other Festivals of Death and Life*, ed. Jack Santino, 133-51. Knoxville: University of Tennessee Press, 1994.

Turner, Kay and Suzanne Seriff. 1987. "Giving an Altar": The Ideology of Reproduction in a St. Joseph's Day Feast. *Journal of American Folklore* 100: 446-61.

Turner, Victor. 1973. The Center Out There: Pilgrim's Goal. *History of Religions* 12: 191-230.

_____. [1969] 1995. *The Ritual Process*. New York: Aldine.

Turner, Victor and Edith Turner. 1978. *Image and Pilgrimage in Christian Culture: Anthropological Perspectives*. New York: Columbia University Press.

Van Gennep, Arnold. 1960. *The Rites of Passage*. Trans. Gabrielle Caffee and Monika B. Vizedom. London: Routledge and Kegan Paul.

Vannatta, Thomas. 1997a. E-mail to the author. 8 July.

_____. 1997b. E-mail to the author. 14 November.

Verhovek, Sam Howe. 1998. 5 years later, battles rage on Koresh legacy: Battles rage around Koresh's legacy 5 years later. *Austin American-Statesman*, 19 April, http://archives.statesman.com

Volkan, Vamik. 1972. The Linking Objects of Pathological Mourners. *Archives of General Psychiatry* 27: 215-221.

Walter, Tony. 1990. Floral Tributes. *Funeral Service Journal*, November, 47-55.

_____, ed. 1999. *The Mourning for Diana*. New York: Berg.

Walter, Tony and Lucy Biddle. 1998. The Emotional English and Their Queen of Hearts. *Folklore* 109: 96-99.

Werchan, James. 1998. Telephone interview by author. 4 March.

West, John O., ed. 1988. *Mexican-American Folklore*. Little Rock: August House.

Wheeler, Maegan. 1997a. Response to "Accident Marker Questionnaire" administered by author. Austin, Texas, 12 May.

_____. 1997b. Telephone interview by author. 1 June.

Whitbeck, Carolyn. 1984. Beyond Domination: New Perspectives on Women and Philosophy. In *A Different Reality: Feminist Ontology*, ed. Carol C. Gould, 64-88. Totowa, NJ: Rowman & Allanheld.

Wimberly, Debbie. 1997a. Response to "Accident Marker Question-naire" administered by author. Austin, Texas, 12 May.

_____. 1997b. Telephone interview by author. 15 May.

Woocher, Jonathan. 1988. Sacred Survival: American Jewry's Civil Religion. *Judaism* 34: 151-62.

Wood, Juliette. 1998. Diana Memorabilia: Mail Order Values in Popular American Magazines. *Folklore* 109: 109-110.

Woolf, Jim. 1996. Crosses Honor Memory of Accident Victims: Old Tradition of Roadside Crosses is Renewed. *Salt Lake Tribune*, 18 May, http://207.179.44.6/96/MAY/18/trl/22243511.htm

Worden, J. William. 1991. *Grief Counseling and Grief Therapy: A Handbook for the Mental Health Practitioner*. New York: Springer.

Wright, Scott W. 1995. Race turns deadly when car hits van. *Austin American-Statesman*, 3 February, http://archives.statesman.com

Young, James E. 1993. *The Texture of Memory: Holocaust Memorials and Meaning*. London: Yale University Press.

Zeitlin, Steven and Ilana Harlow. 2001. How Much of the City's Grief Should We Preserve? *Newsday.com*, 14 October, http://www.newsday.com/news/opinion/ny-vpzeitlin2414071oct14.story

Zimmerman, Thomas. 1997. Sites of Public Death: Roadside Memorials in South Central Kentucky. Paper read at American Folklore Society Annual Meeting, Austin, Texas.

Index